SCHOOLING CHOICES

David W. Smith
Kenneth O. Gangel
Gregg Harris

H. WAYNE HOUSE
Editor

MULTNOMAH

Portland, Oregon 97266

Edited by Jane Aldrich Brown and Rodney L. Morris
Cover design by Judy Quinn

SCHOOLING CHOICES
© 1988 by H. Wayne House
Published by Multnomah Press
Portland, Oregon 97266

Multnomah Press is a ministry of Multnomah School of the Bible, 8435 Northeast Glisan Street, Portland, Oregon 97220.
Printed in the United States of America.

Library of Congress Cataloging-in-Publication Data

Schooling Choices

   Contents: Public school education / David Smith — Christian school education / Kenneth Gangel—Home school education / Gregg Harris.
   1. School, Choice of—United States. 2. Church schools—United States. 3. Public schools—United States. 4. Home schooling—United States. 5. Christian education—United States.
I. House, H. Wayne. II. Smith, David W., 1943-   . III. Gangel, Kenneth O. IV. Harris, Gregg.
LB1027.9.s36   1988   371'.00973   88-25392
ISBN 0-88070-162-5 (pbk.)

88 89 90 91 92 93 94 - 10 9 8 7 6 5 4 3 2 1

In memory of my mother
Sarah Oma Ellen House

CONTENTS

Part 1 Public School Education
David Smith

Part 2 Christian School Education
Kenneth Gangel

Part 3 Home School Education
Gregg Harris

ACKNOWLEDGMENTS

Many people have made significant contributions to the publication of this book. First I would like to thank the authors, David Smith, Kenneth Gangel, and Gregg Harris. They have provided stimulating, and I believe helpful, argumentation for readers who are at a point of decision regarding the education of their children.

My wife Leta helped me by reading the essays and offering many helpful suggestions. Also my sixteen-year-old daughter Carrie read portions of the manuscript. Many thanks to Christi (Dulin) Napier, who volunteered needed office help to free me for tasks such as this book. God bless you Christi! I give my sincere thanks to Michelle Kingry, who read the manuscript in its entirety and gave many useful recommendations for a clearer and more interesting book.

Last of all I wish to thank Jane Aldrich Brown and Rod Morris for their support and patience during a lengthy process, more lengthy than we originally envisioned. They and the staff at Multnomah Press are due special praise.

H. Wayne House

CONTRIBUTORS

Kenneth O. Gangel is professor and chairman of the department of Christian education at Dallas Theological Seminary, Dallas, Texas. He is a graduate of Grace Theological Seminary (M.Div.), Fuller Seminary (M.A.), and the University of Missouri at Kansas City (Ph.D.). Dr. Gangel is a member of the Religious Education Association, the American Association of Higher Education, and the National Association of Professors of Christian Education, and has written numerous books, including *Understanding Teaching* (1968), *Between Christian Parent and Child* (1974), *24 Ways to Improve Your Teaching* (1974), *Building a Christian Family* (1987), and *Christian Education: Its History and Philosophy* (1982). He was twice named one of the Outstanding Educators of America.

Gregg Harris is the founding director of Christian Life Workshops and the author of *The Christian Home School* (1987). He is the author and instructor of various educational programs and materials, including the Home Schooling Workshop, the Family Storytelling Workshop, and most recently the Family Restoration Seminar. Harris's workshops are conducted in over forty major cities each year. Harris is a graduate of Centreville Bible College and studied seminar design and management at the University of Dayton and Wright State University in Dayton, Ohio. He serves as a member of the Private Education Advisory Board to the Governor of the State of Oregon and provides a regular column for *The Teaching Home* magazine. Gregg resides with his wife, Sono, and two sons near Portland, Oregon.

H. Wayne House is assistant professor of systematic theology at Dallas Theological Seminary, Dallas, Texas. He is a graduate of Western Conservative Baptist Seminary (M.Div., Th.M.), Concordia Seminary (Th.D.), and O. W. Coburn School of Law (J.D.), and has taught at Western, Northwestern College, and LeTourneau College. Dr. House is a member of the Evangelical Theological Society, the American Trial Lawyers Association, the American Bar Association, and the Society of Biblical Literature. He has contributed articles to several scholarly journals and has authored *Chronological and Background Charts of the New Testament* (1981) and *Restoring the Constitution* (1987), and co-authored *The Christian Confronts His Culture* (1983) and *Dominion Theology: Blessing or Curse?* (1988).

David W. Smith is superintendent of schools for the Delphi Community School Corporation in Delphi, Indiana. He is a graduate of Bethel College (B.A.), Ball State University (M.A.), and Northwestern University (Ph.D.), and has been a public school educator for twenty years, including twelve years in public high schools in Illinois and Indiana. He is a member of the American Association of School Administrators, the Indiana Association of Public School Superintendents, and the American Association of Supervision and Curriculum Development. Dr. Smith has been a guest on "Focus on the Family" and

NBC's "Today" show, and he is the author of *The Friendless American Male* (1983) and several published articles on education.

The Purpose of This Book

Few decisions have a more lasting impact on your child's life than where he will go to school. From your child's sixth year to his eighteenth, school dominates his life. It shapes his thinking, molds his character, and—to a degree—determines his destiny. But how many parents give much thought to where their children will receive their education and who will give it to them? Too often we allow the conventions of our culture to make that decision for us.

Today's parents have three viable options from which to choose: public school, private school, or home school. Which is best for your child? In *Schooling Choices*, we have let three highly qualified spokesmen have their say so that you, the parent, can make an informed and wise decision.

Schooling Choices draws no final conclusion. No side "wins" or "loses." Our goal is to simply provide you with helpful information and to challenge you to carefully weigh the alternatives. It may be one of the most important decisions you will ever make.

The Publisher

INTRODUCTION

MY wife and I sat in the living room trying to make a difficult decision. Should we send our ten-year-old daughter to a local parochial school, put her back into the public school, or should we teach her at home? We had tried to do all the right things for Carrie. We sent her to preschool, then to a good kindergarten, and finally she began public school a few blocks from our house. The opportunity arose to transfer Carrie to a magnet school in the area that provided "better education for academically qualified applicants." We were proud to be able to get her in. However, it was not long before we recognized that she was not adjusting well. After two years of difficulty we decided we had to make some change.

Such a dilemma is not unusual today. Many parents find themselves in a quandary regarding the education of their children. They want the best education possible for their kids, but they also want to be sure their children receive the proper social and spiritual training. From every corner there are voices urging them to flee the secular public schools. Other voices say to avoid the Christian schools because they are artificial and not beneficial for spiritual growth; children need to be a testimony of Christ to the unsaved in the schools. Additional persons decry the home school movement. Parents are not qualified to teach their children. Professionals have the training and skills to accomplish this task better than parents, although parents should express interest and maintain some type of surveillance over the process.

Rarely will parents be able to evaluate these options in as objective a manner as this book affords. Each of the authors is fully convinced of his position, and each is given the opportunity to respond to the other positions. In this manner, you as a concerned parent may carefully decide which option you prefer for your children after weighing the arguments for each view.

Let me encourage you to consider that no one option may be the best for every child in your family, nor will one be best for any given child their entire educational training. You need to evaluate the age and maturity of the child, the educational capabilities of the child, the quality and kind of public and Christian schools where you live, and your financial situation. We made a decision to evaluate afresh each year our own educational choice. This may also be wise for you.

I believe this book will be of great gain as you seek to fulfill the command of God's Word to train your children and bring them up in the admonition of the Lord.

H. Wayne House

PART 1

PUBLIC
SCHOOL EDUCATION

David Smith

CHAPTER 1

Is There a Biblical Basis for Public Education?

THERE can be no doubt that the Scriptures give the primary responsibility of training children to their parents. Deuteronomy 6:6-9 says that parents are to teach children the ways of God in all contexts of life: when they rise, when they lie down, when they walk together. Proverbs 22:6 says "Train a child in the way he should go." So the matter of who are the primary persons to educate children is not in question. The purpose for this chapter is to show why it is proper for Christian parents to delegate some of the education of children to the public schools.

Some parents consider the public schools as bastions of humanism or anti-God indoctrination centers. Though some teachers may have anti-Christian biases, the overwhelming majority of public schools and our teachers provide positive education that provides an opportunity for Christian students to learn subjects such as science, math, and history. They also give Christian students a chance to live their Christian world view on a daily basis in the classroom.

Christian Influence in Secular Society

Christians are commanded by God to influence and contribute to their society. In order to do this, Christians should not limit their contact to isolated social conclaves where they may be safe and unaffected by society's ills. Instead, Christians are to be light to the world. Jesus says that one does not take a light and put it under a bucket (Luke 8:16). Rather, he puts it on a candlestand to give light to the room. Likewise, Christians should not, as a general rule, take their light and hide it in Christian schools or home schools where it is not able to be brightly and regularly seen by the world. Moreover, Christ said that Christians are to be salt, preserving the world from moral decay. If Christians leave the public schools, then there will be little Christian witness. Before he left the earth, Jesus commanded his followers to go into all the world. Surely this includes involvement with persons in the public schools of America.

The Bible records that we are to be in the world but we are not to be of the world (John 17:15-18). We Christians are not to withdraw from society. Instead, we should meet with those who do not know Christ in all areas of life, including our jobs and our schools. Unfortunately, many Christians have not only adopted much of the world's views but have also withdrawn themselves and their children from the world. Of the world, but not in it.

We see examples of believers in God in the midst of pagan societies in the persons of Joseph and Daniel. Joseph as a teenager was sold into Egyptian slavery. While a slave in Potiphar's house, a prisoner in Pharaoh's prison, and finally a high official in Pharaoh's court, Joseph maintained a witness of honesty, integrity, intelligence, and devotion to God that made a tremendous impact for God and brought many blessings to both the Egyptians and the people of God.

Daniel, as a young man, was taken from his home in Judah by the Babylonians. In the midst of pagans, he had an unblemished testimony and had great influence for God. His religious training at home put him in good stead to stand against the pagan influences he received. His training in secular subjects from the Babylonians gave him ability to be of great service to the Babylonians and later the Medo-Persians, and to his own people Israel.

Student Influence in the Public Schools

Christian students today can take advantage of the education offered in our public schools and thereby be better prepared to serve both man and God. Christians should be the best students possible, both to gain an education for their own development and to contribute spiritually to the lives of other students.

Some have mistakenly thought that Christian students may not practice their religious convictions while at school. This is clearly not the case. While the prayer issue has received the national spotlight, another matter, "equal access," is far more important. The drama of both the school prayer and the equal access issues were played out during 1984 and 1985. While school prayer did not succeed, equal access—the right of students to meet with peers at school to study the Bible and to pray together before or after school—is now guaranteed by law. This new law removes any doubt that students have as much right to congregate to study the Bible as those who wish to study football, Marxism, or chess.

Christian Teachers in Public Schools

While many dedicated Christians work in public schools and possess many First Amendment protections, some tend to be overly cautious. We can teach about the value systems of Marx, Freud, Darwin and others, but Christians are too often hesitant to mention anything biblical, fearing they might somehow violate the Constitution. We need to be a source of encouragement for these teachers.

The Christian Legal Society suggests that Christian teachers follow three general guidelines in exercising their beliefs:

> First, they should treat the children in their classrooms as they would like their own children treated by other teachers of different beliefs. Second, a teacher can answer students' questions. Third, a teacher may discuss his or her personal beliefs when they are relevant to the subject matter.[1]

Several subjects naturally lend themselves to the introduction of religion. History and literature are examples of courses that cannot be taught adequately if religious ideas are censored.

Recently I was invited to speak to four classes of high school seniors taking a family living class. It provided a natural opportunity to speak on topics such as abortion, the sanctity of marriage, the dignity and worth of all people, and the role of authority and submission in the marriage relationship. This was my fifth year speaking to these classes, sharing my world view from a biblical perspective.

Years ago when I was teaching world history I was asked in an interview about my limits for introducing Christianity into my courses. As a public high school social studies teacher I said that there are limitations to using the classroom as a setting for sermons. But I felt fairly free to identify myself as a Christian and to introduce the Christian viewpoint into my lessons.

I do not know how any teacher of history could avoid reference to the impact of Christianity upon the United States and world history. Even with inadequate coverage or secular bias in a textbook, it is easy, and certainly desirable, to supplement the text with other materials and to point out the textbook's anti-Christian assumptions.

Over twenty years ago the Supreme Court said the Bible is worthy of study, and to ignore it would be to ignore one of the major elements that shaped our history and culture. Attorney Samuel Ericsson says, "When people began to say that the Supreme Court expelled God from schools, evangelicals played right into that and lost an opportunity to reach 40 million American school children."[2] Christians need not ask, can we introduce the Bible into the schools? Rather we should ask, how may we best present the Scriptures and Christianity?

In the school where I served as curriculum director we offered an elective Bible course at the high school level. Different points of view were presented fairly. As a result, criticism was almost nonexistent. The course is a study of the Bible, not a practice of, or imposition of, any particular creed. Christian teachers may find creative ways to introduce biblical values and principles, especially within English and social studies. When I taught public school anthropology classes, I had students re-enact the Scopes trial.[3] Students studied both creation and evolution and argued their findings in a courtroom environment. The creationists often won these cases which were judged by students.

Students learn much about the values of their teacher in subtle ways. Does the teacher follow through on promises to the class? Does he return tests and papers within a reasonable time? Does she value honesty and self-control? Does she respect each student? The old cliche that "values are more often caught than taught" is true.

Teachers collectively tend to be a conservative group within our society. They are not the terrible people many Christian and home school advocates portray. The NEA (National Education Association) is far more liberal than the educators it claims to represent. The vast majority of the nearly two million public elementary, middle, and high school teachers are part of the Judeo-Christian tradition. A 1982 Gallup poll indicated that 60 percent of public school teachers believed in the deity of Christ, and 79 percent believed the Bible is the inspired word of God. While some teachers may hold anti-Christian beliefs, no conspiracy exists, even in small numbers, to indoctrinate America's youth.

By the early 1990s, an estimated one million elementary and secondary public school teaching jobs will be open. That is about one-half of America's teachers. We should be encouraging our best and brightest young leaders from our churches and communities to seriously consider public school teaching as a vocation and a ministry.

I am both an evangelical Christian and a public school superintendent. These roles are compatible. I view my vocation as a calling and as a position of civic and Christian service. The two children God has given to my wife and me attend public schools within our community.

Only a handful of the 15,500 school corporations in America are "too far gone" to be successfully changed. In my direct involvement in six school systems, and indirect involvement in dozens of others, I have yet to encounter such a school system. Also, in my observations, a direct correlation exists between the intensity of one's criticism and his lack of involvement with the school being criticized. Involved citizens are less critical and possess fewer misunderstandings.

Christians and individuals possessing Christian principles are present in large numbers in our public schools. This should encourage us as we strive to influence the lives of young people. Numerous Christian students, faculty, administrators, and parents are present and active in our nation's public schools. This multitude has the freedom to influence millions of students and adults who learn and work there. The schools continue to need and deserve our attention and commitment. I believe Christians have reason to be optimistic about their collective role and influence in public education in America.

Chapter 1, Notes
 1. Ken Sidey, "Christ in the Classroom," *Moody Monthly*, March 1986, 27.
 2. Samuel E. Ericsson, "How to Have a Christian Impact in a Public School and Not Get Hauled into Court," *Christianity Today*, 3 February 1984, 61.
 3. David W. Smith, "Scopes Trial Revisited," *Law In American Society: Journal of the National Center for Law Focused Education*, May 1976, 30-34.

CHAPTER 2

How Did Public School Education Begin?

ATTITUDES toward American education have changed dramatically during the last 350 years. While most children today attend neighborhood public schools, schooling for earlier generations was very different. These differences were not limited just to the numbers of children in school but also included what children learned and the methods used to teach them.

There is little doubt that education is different today than in times past. But if parents understand the nature and function of education in today's schools, they will see that it has as much to offer their children as any other form of education in American society.

In this chapter I will briefly look at the rise of early American education and its structure and then compare it with today, tracing the changes that have produced modern American education. Then I will examine the purpose and value of public education.

America's First Public Schools

In 1647 the colony of Massachusetts passed a law requiring each community with at least fifty families to establish a tax-supported elementary school. These schools were available to all children within the community, but apparently attendance was not required. This law served as a model for similar legislation in other American colonies.

Christian training was emphasized in those early elementary schools. The Massachusetts law warned that "the chief project of the old deluder Satan is to keep men from knowledge of scripture." Children were taught to read so they could read the Bible. Teachers emphasized memorization and used harsh discipline.

In addition to the elementary schools, larger communities established Latin grammar schools which were college preparatory institutions for boys. Private academies first appeared in the 1700s, combining practical upper level courses with traditional religion. They were supported by tuition charges and usually admitted only young men. The first public high school, the English High School in Boston, opened its doors in 1821.

After the Revolution, American education gradually began to change. While still concerned with religious education, Americans became increasingly involved with the problems of building a new unified nation. Immigrants were entering the United States from many diverse cultural backgrounds, and a common language and a sense of patriotism became important educational objectives. Vocational training was also instituted during this time.

The nineteenth century was a time of tremendous change in America as the country quickly moved from a rural nation to an industrial world power. Many Americans believed the existing schools—the Latin schools, academies, and an assortment of parochial schools—could not measure up to the difficult task of educating the nation's youth. This led to what has been called the "Common School Crusade."

Reformers such as Horace Mann in Massachusetts and Henry Barnard in Connecticut were appalled by the poor quality of schools and the poor attendance of the children. They argued that education for every child, supported with tax dollars, was actually an investment in the economy. An educated person would contribute to, rather than drain, economic resources. Soon free compulsory public elementary schools sprang up across New England and over the Appalachians, sparked also by the fear that there existed a potential danger of lawlessness when diverse people were left without instruction in basic values and literacy. Formal public education was the recipe which would make people productive, honest, law-abiding American citizens.

The Secularization of Public Education

Most educational reformers of the early nineteenth century still believed public schools should have Bible reading and religious instruction as an aid to good citizenship. The millions who arrived from the Old World enrolled their children in a new public school system that favored conservative Protestant Christianity. Several groups, including Catholics, Lutherans, and Jews, wanted the schools to be religiously neutral, devoted to character building and patriotism.

Roman Catholics reacted to the anti-Catholic sentiment present within many schools of the time. In many communities, Protestants responded by making education more secular. In other communities, some Catholics, believing schools to be hopelessly Protestant, began private, sectarian schools. Neither Protestants nor Catholics desired to make public schools less religiously oriented, but the disagreements between them ironically led to just that.

Wealthy citizens were troubled with the idea of universal public education, in which all strata of children would be educated, because they perceived that it attempted to equalize everyone. Many families of means continued to send their children to private schools.

On the other hand, the lower classes and the growing middle class were convinced that education was essential to pursuing the American Dream. They reflected the thinking of Thomas Jefferson, who believed that public schools would lead America to an "aristocracy of talent rather than of inherited wealth and privilege."[1] The public schools have aided the breakdown of social class barriers and increased the opportunity for all citizens, regardless of religion, race, or social status, to succeed in America. By World War I, each state had laws requiring every child to attend school.

The Changing Purpose of Public Education

Schools have continued to change in recent decades. For example, in 1954 the Supreme Court ruled in the famous Brown decision that it was unconstitutional for schools to restrict Negroes from attending with whites. And in 1965, Congress passed the Elementary and Secondary Education Act which provided money to improve schools in disadvantaged neighborhoods. Integration, poverty, and underachievement are still concerns of public schools in the late 1980s.

Americans continue to turn to their public schools for solutions to new and old social needs. Schools are asked to desegregate, immunize, feed, counsel, nurse, care for the handicapped, train athletes, and provide bilingual and bicultural career, drug, sex, global, and values education along with instruction in physical hygiene. This is all in addition to the task of passing on to each new generation basic English, math, social studies, and science knowledge.

Public schools have been asked to assume this vast range of responsibilities largely because of the diminishing influence of both the church and the family. We all need to be concerned with how public schools can best respond to student and social problems such as spiraling divorce rates, teenage pregnancy, abortion, single-parent families, drug abuse, suicide, permissiveness, unemployment, social injustice, child abuse, and child neglect. Schools, which were created to perform a few basic functions, are now being asked to perform dozens of them.

Public schools are performing a vital function for all Americans. Schools instruct students in personality development, vocational training, character and values formation, knowledge acquisition, and citizenship training. Public schools assume all these important responsibilities and more.

Public schools alone cannot meet the challenges and needs of today's children. Other institutions, primarily the church and family, must assume more responsibility for the social, educational, and spiritual well-being of children.

Indeed, if public schools are to contribute measurably to the lives of young Americans, they will require a narrower purpose and the cooperation of church, family, and community.

What, then, is the primary purpose of public education in contemporary society? This is well answered by former Secretary of Education T. H. Bell in a 1983 speech to the National Forum on Excellence in Education:

> The first priority—taking precedence over all else that we do—is to concentrate on the attainment by every student of the highest possible level of literacy so that each student will have reached the outer limits of his or her ability to read with comprehension, write and think systematically and logically, and to speak with clarity in a manner that is

articulate, precise, and reflective of an intelligent, well-educated individual. This priority should be number one, and the schools of this nation must make a fully unambiguous commitment to its attainment.[2]

Chapter 2, Notes
  1. Letter from Thomas Jefferson to John Adams on 28 October 1813, John Bartlett, *Familiar Quotations* (Boston: Little, Brown and Co., 1980), 389.
  2. I was present to hear Dr. Bell give this speech on 8 December 1983 in Indianapolis. An unpublished paper of his remarks was available that day and was entitled, "Suggested Priorities and Goals for American Education," National Forum on Excellence in Education.

CHAPTER 3

What Are the Spiritual Advantages of a Public School Education?

IN the public schools young people can develop a mature Christian life which will stand up against the challenges of adolescence. Real life circumstances can build a confident Christian.

A pharmacist who recently removed his middle-school-aged children from a Christian school told me,

> Many tried to give me a guilt trip when I returned my kids to the public school. But before God and man, I believe we have made the correct decision. I now feel more directly responsible for the spiritual education of my children, not the church school professionals. I feel that the children are now growing in their faith, and when we attend church the services are more meaningful to us.

Another parent I talked with in Minneapolis told me,

> Sure our kids will hear and even experience ideas
> that they don't agree with. But I'd much rather have
> them struggle with these conflicts while still under
> my roof and direct leadership. At least they can
> come home and discuss their events of the public
> school day. The result of dealing with ideas different
> from their own is that they begin to think and begin
> to apply their biblical values to everyday cir-
> cumstances. As they begin to think Christianly their
> faith becomes their own.

Doug Haag is the youth pastor at the First Evangelical Free Church in Fullerton, California. One evening, following a seminar I presented at his church, Doug
and a few church members were discussing what kind of
schools Christian kids should attend. Pastor Haag told
me that Christian school students often develop a cloistered mentality: "They don't see living in the community
as a spiritual challenge." Doug believes students attending Christian high schools reach the conclusion that their
parents sent them there because they cannot handle the
world and have no trust in their ability to live and think
Christianly.

Christian Students in Public School

Children should face the tough issues while they
are at home where parents can seize the opportunity to
coach them, rather than years later at college or work
when the consequences for wrong choices are much more
grave.

We need to trust our children and to encourage
them to demonstrate the teachings they hear at home
and at church. If we take an interest in others and have
confidence in ourselves and in the power of God's promises, we and our children can serve and influence others.

A fifth-grade boy sitting next to my daughter during lunch at school began to cry. Julie talked with him and learned that his parents were going through a divorce. Julie became his friend and was a help to this boy, primarily because she listens well. Julie is a more sensitive person now because she tries to be open to classmates who are having problems.

When my wife Sue Ann and I were junior and senior high school youth sponsors at a Bible church in Des Plaines, Illinois, we found that students from public schools were the best leaders in church ministries. We found two reasons for the spirituality of public school teens.

- They have their faith tested daily and are hungry for truth and support.
- They have friends who are not Christians, and they are concerned for these people they love.

Many Christian school students are simply "churched out." They have had their Christian fellowship needs met and have been formally force-fed Bible all week long at church school. The kids in our church youth group who attended Christian schools often lacked interest in both Bible study and activities with kids who were a little different socially or spiritually from themselves.

I asked a middle-aged couple about the spiritual aspect of sending their four children to public schools. They said,

When Jesus spoke of the need for Christians to be the salt, He didn't mean we were to be mounds of salt. When we salt our food we don't pile all the salt upon one area of our dinner plate. If we remove all "salt" from our public schools, we should not complain about what is left. The Holy Spirit of God can only do His work in these schools through the lives of those He inhabits—students, faculty, and staff. Jesus said, 'You will be my witnesses' (Acts 1:8).

Christian students have the responsibility and the privilege to be this power for good of which Jesus taught. Of course, there will be times a Christian student will feel discouraged. We as parents need to take a periodic inventory of our participation in public school. During the discouraging times, we need to ask ourselves what the outcome would be if all Christian students and teachers left our public schools. If this were to happen, the evangelical community would lose its potential influence with the overwhelming majority of this nation's children who are not attending either the Christian schools or home schools. The public schools are the most strategic place where committed Christians can affect the world.

We Christians need to prepare our children at home and at church to deal with secular reasoning, theories, and arguments that conflict with genuinely biblical teachings. Children will encounter false philosophies in school, but an open environment where children are free to ask difficult questions provides a super opportunity to explore each philosophy, each idea, logically in light of biblical realities. This is how people acquire and practice biblical faith.

Secular issues and arguments should not be ignored. God is the author of all truth. Jesus said, "You will know the truth, and the truth will set you free" (John 8:32). Without being defensive, we should be willing to confront biblically any question or concern our children wish to pursue or that their school has thrust upon them. When students attend public schools, homes and churches should assume more responsibility for their instruction in Christian beliefs and behavior.

Unfortunately, too often many conservative fundamentalists want to retreat rather than to confront the social and religious issues affecting our society.

Unexpected Outcomes

Many involved in establishing new Christian academy schools are far more conservative than most Christians. Many of these anti-public school conservatives live in what Leslie K. Tarr, an evangelical pastor, once referred to as a hermetically sealed world.[1] Dr. Tarr believes that this group is busy erecting high emotional walls between themselves and the larger evangelical community. They tend to share many traits—for example, defensiveness, narrowness, authoritarianism—which can seriously hinder an impressionable young person's spiritual and educational development.

Christian schools which teach that there is but one position, only one right way to think and believe on any and every subject have imposed a great burden upon themselves. These school administrators believe that the way they think is the way all people, churches, and schools should think. Disagreement is frowned upon. Honest differences of opinion expressed sincerely are dismissed as false and even sinful. Many church and home school groups are apparently interested in preparing students who will be isolated from society. These students will fail to see the need for compromise and will believe that limiting experiences is good for everyone. It is not the purpose of public schools to prepare students who think this way.

A Parent's Decision

If we enter the public school expecting to find able, caring people, we will likely find them. It is far more productive to personally find out what is going on in your children's local school than to read books such as Phyllis Schlafly's *Child Abuse in the Classroom* or Tim LaHaye's *The Battle for the Public Schools* and simply assume the very worst about your neighborhood school. We should rely on our own local investigation. This will be far more accurate and fruitful than relying upon generalizations made by well-meaning Christian leaders.

I believe I have a responsibility both as a Christian and as an American citizen to support and influence the public schools. I believe also that in the majority of circumstances children from godly homes and Christ-honoring churches will function well in the public school arena.

I want to say, however, that there is no absolutely correct answer to where a parent should enroll a daughter or a son. No two children will respond precisely the same way to the same set of circumstances. Neighborhoods differ, as do parents, churches, schools, peers, siblings, relatives, and children themselves. In some circumstances it would be best for a child to attend public school; in others, a Christian or home school might be preferable. For those who have departed from the public school, I hope they will understand and respect the thinking and the spirituality of those parents who have chosen to remain in public education.

Parents must evaluate social and spiritual circumstances along with the specific characteristics of their children before they reach a decision. Parents, and parents alone, can make the proper decision of where their children attend school, for they alone know best the environmental circumstances and the temperament and individual traits of each of their own children.

Chapter 3, Notes
   1. Leslie K. Tarr, "The Hermetically Sealed World of Neo- Fundamentalism," *Eternity*, August 1976, 24-27.

CHAPTER 4

Are There Educational Advantages to Public Schools?

BOTH of my children are enrolled in the public schools of our community. Julie and Cameron attend these neighborhood schools because Sue Ann and I believe they will acquire skills, knowledge, and attitudes essential for living a life that is productive, purposeful, and pleasing to God.

My parents had the same hopes for me as I do for my children. My parents, Eveline and William H. Smith, were both children of German immigrants. My grandparents came to this great country from northern Germany with only a dream of a better life for themselves and their children.

Living on Chicago's north side during the Depression, my parents worked tirelessly just to keep food on the table. For nearly forty years my Dad was a faithful employee of the Borden Dairy in Skokie, Illinois. My working-class parents looked to the public schools, not as a cure-all, but as an opportunity for their children to acquire a quality education. As a result of their confidence and support, I was given the opportunity and privilege of attending for twelve years the local public schools of Wilmette and Winnetka, Illinois.

My public school experience as a student was in the 1950s and 1960s. Many today believe that schools provided a better education years ago. We hear that public school education was better in the good old days. This myth has been with us for some time. A generation ago, Will Rogers said, "Schools aren't as good as they used to be, but they never were." Earlier periods of history have always been targets of romantic generalizations.

Equal Educational Opportunity

All children, regardless of their background or ability, are admitted on an equal basis to our public schools. This integral experiment in democracy, the burdens notwithstanding, has been and continues to be a success.

In 1900, only 6 percent of the population acquired a high school diploma.[1] Today 80 percent are educated to that level.[2] Research indicates that the average student today is more proficient at both reading and computing than students of earlier generations.[3] There are nearly forty million children enrolled in American public elementary and secondary schools.[4] In most cases these students, America's future, are receiving a good education.

While much work still needs to be done, the literacy rate today is much higher than in earlier years. Despite current economic problems, including major competition from nations such as Japan, our industrial achievements remain the envy of millions around the world. Our social and economic accomplishments would not have occurred had America not made a commitment to education for all of its citizens without regard to religion, race, or social class.

How does American education compare with the educational systems of other industrial nations? Dr.

Torstein Husen, in his role as chairman of the International Association for the Evaluation of Achievement (IEA), has for twenty-five years been directly involved in cross-national educational research. Dr. Husen concludes that it is difficult to make valid cross-national comparisons of student achievement. Often on standardized tests an elite few in certain countries are compared with large numbers of Americans. In one mathematics study, fewer than 10 percent of the students in selected European countries were compared with more than 70 percent of the students in the United States.[5]

There is no point in making comparisons of student performances representing highly different proportions of a certain age group. When you compare equal proportions of age groups, American students perform at least as well as their counterparts in other industrialized nations. Standards of average performance can easily be raised when a system is made more selective. It is a lot easier to provide excellent education if you are only going to educate relatively few children, especially if they are students who already do well. If the schools try to educate all children, the job becomes more difficult.

In comparing students and educational systems, we should ask how many students are brought how far. France has admitted that little Jacques cannot read very well. In 1985 a very critical education report was issued by the French study group, Organization for Economic Cooperation and Development. The French system of education, which is similar to that of other European nations, selects and trains well only the best students. This shortchanges the less able. At a young age, a few children are tracked into a good education and the majority receive a far less adequate education.

While European educational systems have neglected the great majority of students in an effort to educate a selected few, they are beginning to emulate America's comprehensive system with its broader access and higher retention rates.

Competitive Academic Achievement

During the last fifteen years, America's public schools have assimilated fifteen million immigrants. This is one of the largest immigration waves in our history. Public schools have been the key mechanism for fitting these immigrants into our society.

In recent years American educators have been hearing a great deal about the growing superiority of Japanese schools. Public school critic Mortimer Adler, chairman of the board of editors of *Encyclopaedia Britannica*, told reporters recently in Tokyo "Japan is doing better than we are because of its longer school year, better pay for teachers, more respect for teachers and hard work by students." Adler has not mentioned the relatively higher suicide rates among Japanese students. Nor does he mention the lack of attention devoted to critical thinking skills in Japan.

A recent book by Merry White[6] suggests that the success of Japanese schools is rooted not so much in their educational policies as in cultural traditions. In Japan there is enormous social pressure to fit into groups, to be accepted. Parents in Japan, in contrast with Americans, attach greater importance to hard work than to basic ability in determining academic success.

In addition to international comparisons, American public schools have also been compared to private schools in this country. Dr. James Coleman of the University of Chicago, in his controversial 1982 report, concluded that traditional long-standing private schools may be doing a better job than public schools.[7] We have known for generations that the larger established private schools have done a good job of educating children. Little is known, however, about the newer, smaller, fundamentalist Christian academies.

Coleman also mentions that most children enrolled in private schools come from affluent middle-class homes that place a high value on education. One would expect these children to do well regardless of the type of school they attend.

More recently researchers at the University of California at Davis have concluded that there is no difference between the academic achievements of private and public school students. The study compared two groups of students matched for background, gender, age, ethnicity, and ability. It concluded that private and public schooling has, on the average, about the same influence on academic achievement in reading and mathematics.

While private school students may be better off financially and better motivated, it would appear the public schools are able to hold their own, despite having to enroll any student, good or bad.

In most communities the public schools provide quality education. This is not to deny that problems exist. Problems exist in every institution in America, including the government and churches.

For the overwhelming majority of children, however, the public schools offer the best teaching techniques, the best curriculum, and the best extracurricular opportunities: in short, the most comprehensive education available.

Chapter 4, Notes
1. Thomas Jones and David Tyack, "Learning from Past Efforts to Reform the High School," *Phi Delta Kappan*, February 1983, 403.
2. Ibid.
3. Harold Hodgkinson, "What's Right with Education?" *Phi Delta Kappan*, November 1979, 160.
4. "Digest of Educational Statistics, 1985-1986," Office of Educational Research and Improvement, U.S. Dept. of Education, Center for Statistics, Washington, D.C., 7.
5. Torstein Husen, *The School in Question: A Comparative Study of School and Its Future in Western Societies* (New York: Oxford University Press, 1979).
6. Merry White, *The Japanese Educational Challenge: A Commitment to Children* (New York: Free Press, 1987).
7. James Coleman, Thomas Hoffer, and Sally Kilgore, *High School Achievement: Public, Catholic, and Private Schools Compared* (New York: Basic Books, 1982).

CHAPTER 5

How Will Our Children Benefit Socially from a Public School?

"CHRISTIANS in public schools will be pulled down to the level of the other kids."

"Public schools are too far gone. Secular humanism is everywhere."

"Morals are out. They teach and do anything that feels good in public schools."

Are these realistic concerns, or do they demonstrate a lack of faith that Christian children can have a positive influence for good and can develop spiritually while enrolled in a public school? In some communities these fears may be realistic. In most schools they are unjustified.

It is virtually impossible to isolate ourselves and our children completely from evil people (1 Corinthians 5:10). And is isolation desirable? Has not the Bible given us assurance that God is with us? During the Great Depression, Franklin D. Roosevelt said, "The only thing we have to fear is fear itself." Our fears, often unconscious, tend to paralyze us, preventing the possibility of growth. But "God has not given us the spirit of fear but . . . of a sound mind" (2 Timothy 1:7, KJV).

Just a little light will have a great influence upon darkness. Is not this our calling—to be involved with our social world, to change our world for good (Matthew 5:14-16)?

Go into the World

Our secular society needs a legitimate Christian witness that is not afraid to tackle the many difficult problems facing all Americans. There is a place for Christians of all ages in every realm of our society, including the public schools. Our children benefit socially from this real-life participation.

It is time to end a Christian faith that is ineffective and limited solely to the private places of home and church and is not expected to have any influence upon how we think and act at school, at work, or at any government or cultural function. This ghettoizing, or isolating, of Christian faith is unnatural, and our children know it is unnatural.

And yet the mere mention of "pluralism" or "the separation of church and state" or "forcing your morality upon others" often frightens many Christians. Instead of being defensive and critical, we as Christian parents, citizens, and students have a responsibility to become better informed of our rights, which will enable us to better represent our values.

The church often has failed to help us learn how to live in society as Christians. Many people are turned off to religion because it does not seem real or relevant. Frequently sermon topics are irrelevant or reactionary or both. Quoting from a recent Gallup Poll, *Focus on the Family* magazine[1] concludes that Americans are losing trust in the nation's churches. In 1987, only 57 percent of Americans expressed confidence in churches—down from 66 percent in 1985. This drop in confidence was recorded prior to the scandals and controversy with different well-known television preachers.

During the nineteenth century, evangelicals were involved in every aspect of social life. Their influence made a difference in this country's development. It was these evangelicals of an earlier day who led the fight for the removal of slavery, the development of public education, and legislation to protect women and children.[2] These fellow believers of an earlier generation helped to maintain a high-level biblical view of mankind. Their traditional values were the values of the majority. Children could easily observe and personally know that Christianity was real and relevant.

Christians alive today, at the end of the twentieth century, can reclaim for our culture the heritage of biblical values that was the legacy of our evangelical forefathers. We still live in a free society and we still possess the ability to share with others the hope that is within us. Unlike much of the world, Americans have freedom. We therefore have the responsibility to be both salt and light in the social world in which we and our children live and work and attend school.

A Moral Climate

When in attendance at neighborhood public schools, our children experience a sense of reality. They know that they will learn from others. They know also that they have something to share with others.

Thousands of liberal, moderate, and conservative Christians are teaching within our schools. Millions of Christian children are attending public schools. Together, Christians of all ages can encourage a moral climate with their manner of life, and in appropriate situations they can share both the reality of and the reason for their faith. These Christians may exert a moral influence upon all children within our public schools. Values can be conveyed both in and outside the classroom by teachers, administrators, students, and citizens in general.

In addition to opposing secularism or humanism, many Christian and home schools are also opposed to historical humanism, which recognizes both the dignity of man and the importance of culture. This opposition is strange in that Christians have for centuries accepted the value of humanism, which includes the study of art, literature, history, culture, and civilization. In public schools, our children are taught the history and the culture of the Western world. Christian and Jewish thought have contributed greatly to our history and culture. Christians of earlier periods, rather than denying or ignoring their culture, instead created and used it as a vehicle to express their faith. In public schools children learn about this rich cultural heritage.

Schools can and do place an emphasis upon the heritage, values, and beliefs that unite us as Americans. The responsibility of public school educators is to teach and model the important character traits and national values where there is agreement, not to concentrate upon deeply held convictions which divide us as Americans. The emphasis is upon cooperation rather than disagreement, upon compromise rather than strife. Our children are beneficiaries of and participants in this daily exercise in democracy.

Despite our cultural and religious differences, we as Americans agree with a wide range of values that are of major importance on the public school agenda. Charles L. Glenn, a state-level public school official in Massachusetts, believes that most American parents

> want their children to be kind and compassionate, respectful of the rights of others, and able to listen to differing views while still standing up for their own convictions. I believe that American parents want their children to be truthful, loyal, and committed to the good of society. I believe they want them to love their country and to be committed to its political system and to the rule of law rather than

of men. We may differ vastly on "the highest good," but we agree more than we may think on what qualities we would like our children to have.[3]

In this public environment of tolerance, which places emphasis upon positive consensus, our children can learn how to get along with others. They learn to avoid extremism. Our children learn from children who may be different from them. Moreover, they learn how to influence others constructively.

Children develop best in a social world which they believe is both real and relevant. Anything less does not satisfy them or encourage spiritual growth. The public schools provide Christian students with the opportunity to develop Christian character in an atmosphere that is not artificial. It offers responsibilities and real-life solutions to problems.

Chapter 5, Notes

1. *Focus on the Family*, April 1987, 10.
2. David Moberg, *The Great Reversal: Evangelicals and Social Concern* (New York: J. B. Lippincott, 1977).
3. Charles L. Glenn, "What Evangelicals Should Expect of Public Schools," *The Reformed Journal*, September 1986, 16.

CHAPTER 6

How Will Our Family Benefit from Enrolling Our Child in a Public School?

THE majority of Christian parents have made a conscious decision to send their children to the local public school. Many of these parents believe that enrollment in a Christian school would isolate themselves and their children. It would be counterproductive and perhaps even in opposition to principles set forth in the Bible. Home school, too, is viewed by many as a social isolation and is often dismissed as an unacceptable and unnecessary option.

Education Begins at Home

Schools are not addressed in Ephesians 6:4, where Paul informs parents that their ultimate responsibility to their children is to "bring them up in the training and instruction of the Lord." Moses also, in Deuteronomy 6:6-7, leaves no doubt that child-rearing responsibilities reside finally with parents. Public schools should reinforce purposeful discipline and character development acquired at home, but the major responsibility resides with parents. When Eli failed to discipline his sons for their immoral behavior, God held Eli himself responsible (1 Samuel 3:13).

We cannot delegate the primary parenting role to the church or school. Those involved in home schooling are aware of this potential danger and believe that some parents may be lulled into a false sense of security by enrolling their children in Christian schools. Home school parents are equally aware of the danger of sending children to public schools and abandoning them, by lack of interest and involvement, to whatever social forces prevail at school.

We as parents are in a position to have overwhelming influence on the educational, social, and spiritual development of our sons and daughters who have been entrusted to us by God. Rarely is the key the school they attend. Rather, the key to reaching out to our children, to taking our parenting responsibilities seriously, is to budget time, concern, and emotional commitment, consciously and purposefully, for each of our children.

My wife and I have asked my sister-in-law and her husband to serve as guardians of our children should we die before Julie and Cameron reach adulthood. We are grateful that they have consented to assume this responsibility. Ron is an assistant pastor and Mimi is a teacher in a Christian school. I have told my in-laws that we have much peace in knowing that our children would be raised by a caring family that would love them and instruct them in the Christian faith. Where our children would attend school is of secondary importance. A good Christian home is the most important influence in a child's life.

Each school day morning, my wife, Sue Ann, has a few brief minutes of prayer and discussion with Julie and Cameron about the anticipated school day before they go out the door and onto the school bus. They thank God for the new day and its opportunities and challenges. They talk about being prepared with completed homework and how God wants them to think and behave. Also, at the end of the day, time is set aside to discuss school and other experiences of the day. We both look forward to these scheduled daily times with our children.

Typical questions are "Cameron, how might you respond when another child crowds ahead of you in line?" "Julie, what should you do or say when some children are making fun of the girl in your room who wears glasses and is real skinny?" On a matter we had to deal with recently, Sue Ann asked, "Julie, let's ask God for wisdom on how to respond to your teacher who thinks that creation is a myth." Advance planning can alleviate many problems with which your children will be confronted.

Parent Involvement

As a parent it's important to get to know your children's local school as soon as they enter kindergarten. Some parents are willing to send their children off to spend every weekday with adults who are largely strangers. Many teachers find this puzzling and are irritated by this lack of interest on the part of many parents.

It is never too late to get involved, even if your children are now teenagers. Make it known to teachers, administrators, and your children that you are a concerned, cooperating parent who is interested in working with them in a team approach for the well-being of your children and their school.

In nearly every situation, both parent and teacher want children to succeed. And success is more likely when home and school work together. Your kids will appreciate the support from home, too. I remember my daughter telling me, "Dad, I think it's neat that you and Mom know my principal, Mr. Harber, and my teacher, Mrs. Williams." Children benefit from the sense of security that comes from knowing that school and home are working together on their behalf.

Sue Ann is tutoring a boy in Julie's school who is having reading and self-esteem problems. Once a week, Sue Ann works with this boy and his teacher in an effort to improve his academic skills and feelings about himself. In my son's school, she was asked to spend one hour a week tutoring in English a student who recently arrived from Korea. As a result of this tutoring, Sue Ann has experienced informal and friendly conversations with several teachers, including our children's teachers. Julie and Cameron appreciate seeing their mom at school. And Sue Ann feels a sense of satisfaction in being able to help, even if it is just two hours a week.

We should ask questions of teachers which will help us better understand our children's school environment and learning needs. If you are concerned you might forget to ask an important question, make a list and take it with you when you meet with teachers. Most teachers will be happy to answer questions such as the following:

- Is my child working to the level of his ability?
- What kind of groups is he assigned to and why?
- What kind of textbooks and teaching procedures do you use?
- What is your approach to homework, and how can I help at home?
- How is my child doing in his different subjects?
- Is my child well behaved? What is your discipline policy?

During your scheduled meeting with the teacher, you may need to share personal information about your child that will help in meeting individual needs in the classroom. Mention to the teacher any physical disabilities or other problems your child has that may complicate or alter his or her learning. The teacher will also like to know about the home environment and special interests and abilities.

As a matter of routine, you will receive report cards and have opportunities to schedule parent conferences.

But you and the teacher may need and want additional communication. I am thinking about a flesh-and-blood relationship where parent and teacher know each other. Everybody is busy, but this relationship need not require a great deal of time.

We expect a great deal of our teachers. We need also to expect a great deal of ourselves. We can benefit from a list of reasonable behaviors which teachers may expect from us as parents.

During 1986 and 1987 I had the privilege of working with teachers, administrators, parents, students, and school board members on this issue of expectations. This large group concluded that everyone in the community has a stake in, and is in some way responsible for, both instruction and learning.

This is teamwork involving the family and the school. Schools need to provide all students with opportunities to succeed to the level of their abilities. The school needs to assist students with the vital task of mastering basic life skills. Schools must monitor progress and communicate with parents regularly. And students, of course, must be expected to make the most of their learning opportunities.

What Schools Expect of Parents

Children and their schools also need the direct participation of parents if students are going to be successful. Parents, in a sense, are making a contract with the school agreeing that education is a team effort. The parent committee in my school system prepared a long list of expectations they felt were important and directly related to successful learning. Many of the parental responsibilities that our local parents agreed to are listed below.

- Plan for parent/child and parent/teacher communication.
- Be aware of, and become part of, your child's interests.

- Schedule at least one hour a week with each child alone.
- Do not send a sick child to school.
- Support PTA and other school organizations.
- Become an active citizen in your community.
- Get to know your child's friends and their parents.
- Attend school and city functions.
- Subscribe to and encourage family reading of magazines and newspapers.
- Take advantage of educational resources in the metropolitan area, for example, museums, the arts, and music.
- Use the local library.
- Read to and with your child. Encourage reading.
- Make sure homework is completed. Check daily. Provide a quiet place and time for homework.
- Provide encouragement to raise self-esteem.
- Assign tasks and responsibilities to foster independence and responsibility.
- Recognize both strengths and weaknesses in each child.
- Avoid comparisons between children.
- Develop respect for authority at school and in life.
- Display a positive attitude toward education.
- Remember the need for play time.
- Give your children a hug daily and let them know they are accepted and loved.
- Monitor quality and quantity of television.
- Help the child develop a positive attitude about school, learning, life, and self.
- Support the school with its task of maintaining discipline.
- Encourage pride in our school, state, and country.
- Do not be afraid to say no.
- Set limits and rules.
- Insist upon regular attendance at school.
- Prepare students for learning with proper dress, grooming, nutrition, and rest.

• Teach citizenship, morality, and character.

Family involvement and responsibility are the keys to success. Parenting is not a passive or non-participant responsibility. With family involvement we can help our children, our children's school, and the community as a whole.

CHAPTER 7

How Does Public School Education Help Society?

AMERICANS still share many important core values. This is true despite the media attention highlighting our national differences. Since their founding, our public schools have been basic to national unity. In thousands of schools our national motto, *e pluribus unum,* "Out of Many, One," is lived out on a daily basis.

Our schools have helped support basic traditional values. Teachers share them with each new generation of Americans. The idea of a melting pot, the bringing together and binding together of diverse people, took form and is furthered in the public schools of America.

The tradition of public education is rooted in compromise and cooperation in each local community. Today many Christians are departing from this tradition of Americans working together with tolerance despite differences. The new Christian schools and home schools are established by well-meaning people who, I believe, assume they can have little or no influence within our culture, including public schools. This is not true. In this democracy, citizens have the opportunity, the right, and even the responsibility to influence our schools.

Public Schools and American Democracy

Problems inevitably occurred for earlier generations of Americans when Protestants, Catholics, and Jews came together in the public school classrooms. But by attending school together, children began to see fellow students as individuals. Religious and social class prejudice and bigotry were muted somewhat. Public schools were a common ground where children of different backgrounds came together, learned each other's names, and became Americans together.

Stereotypes and prejudices were not wiped out completely. The nineteenth century had many occasions of religious and class-oriented hatred and violence. With the exception of the Civil War, however, this nation has remained united for more than two hundred years. This was not a foregone conclusion. Eighteenth- century Europeans were convinced our experiment with democracy would soon fail. After the birth of the United States, Benjamin Franklin said only partially in jest, "We have a republic, if we can keep it."

Holy wars have been averted in this great nation. This is not a fact to be taken lightly. The daily newspapers remind us that our toleration of differences is not commonplace on the world stage.

A 1988 Haitian election day ended with widespread violence and murder. Central America and parts of Asia are in the midst of tragic civil wars. And the Middle East has experienced one tragedy after another for years. The people of Northern Ireland still use the terms of religious warfare. Protestants and Catholics there attend separate schools, read separate newspapers, and work in separate shops and factories. Some Protestants and Catholics actually fight and kill each other—often in the name of Christ.

Holy wars and political wars are ablaze around the world. Americans are being held hostage by Islamic extremists in the Middle East. The tragic murders by terrorists of innocent people on ships and in European airports has become all too common in recent years. Today, all over the world, people are killing their fellow humans, often in the name of religion.

The day following the 1984 American presidential election, Robert Strauss, then chairman of the Democratic Party, was interviewed on ABC's "Good Morning America." His words tell us much about our wonderful country. "We're all winners. Here I am, a member of the opposition, being interviewed for my opinion on national television. In Russia, I'd be under house arrest. The only losers are the non-voters who missed participating." How different it was in the 1986 presidential election in the Philippines. At least two dozen of Corazon Aquino's campaign leaders were murdered. President Ferdinand Marcos used fraud and terrorism in an unsuccessful effort to keep himself in office.

How does America avoid the political instability that is so common in much of the world? One major factor, I believe, has been our public schools, which are available to all our children without regard to religion, race, or social standing. In public schools, children learn to be responsible as citizens. They learn tolerance, which prevents being socially narrow. The direct relationship between free schools and a free people was an obvious truth to earlier generations.

Although unrealistic expectations were, and still are, heaped at the schoolhouse door, nevertheless American schools have gone a long way toward narrowing the gap between rich and poor, well-informed and ignorant. Our schools have done a remarkable job in easing the road to upward mobility. Compared to any other industrialized nation, a far greater percentage of America's poor make significant academic achievements, which are usually a prerequisite for economic and social success. This democratic view is vital to maintaining political and economic stability and is reminiscent of the goals in early days of public education.

Many Things to Many People

Despite successes, educators and parents remain disillusioned and are now admitting that education cannot solve all problems. Education alone never will be a cure-all for emotional, spiritual, and social problems. This is especially true for spiritual concerns. Education is an important ingredient in the solution of personal or social issues, but it can only be part of the answer.

Public schools have been asked, with monotonous regularity, to combat problems which logically lie outside the realm of education. The schools have been called upon to help stop drug abuse, reduce highway fatalities by training good drivers, entertain the public with sports and plays, fight venereal disease and AIDS, reduce racial injustice, and conduct charitable drives. The list of expectations seems endless. It appears that every problem that comes along is declared an educational problem, and the public schools are assigned the task of solving it.

This is a significant tribute to the public schools of America. It highlights a history of success. Schools have had an impact in the past on many issues of concern to Americans. But even in the best of times the public schools are vulnerable to criticism, due largely to their visibility. Each day children return home with a report of the events at school.

Criticism of Public Schools

In earlier generations, our schools were responsible mainly for the teaching of reading and computation skills—the basics that many say we should go back to. The church, the home, and the community handled the other important aspects of children's development. No longer! Schools are under increasing pressure to be substitute parents as the traditional family continues to disintegrate. Parents are looking for schools to teach manners, morals, sexual attitudes, health, and other subjects which by tradition have been the domain of the family and the church.

Instead of recognizing their own responsibilities, many people, including Christian parents and churches, are blaming the public schools for every form of social and religious problem. We're told by many Christians and by some educational reform reports, such as the 1983 "Nation at Risk," that the schools have failed our children to the point that our national security is threatened. Xerox president David Kearnes sent an open letter to each 1988 presidential candidate bluntly blaming public schools for turning out workers with a "50 percent defect rate." Xerox expects "100 percent defect-free parts from our suppliers," he said. But the industrial model cannot work for developing the minds of young people. Ken Tyson, a public school educator, says, "Xerox would reject children who are worried about family problems; poorly dressed; nutritionally deficient; sick or tired; mentally handicapped; . . . physically handicapped; abused, neglected, or delinquent; grieving; or in love."[1]

Many offer a simple "quick fix" that will save our schools. Teachers, scolded by armchair critics, are told to straighten up and get back to basics if we are to end our national crisis of illiteracy. These statements cause only misunderstandings and fear.

More people die in hospitals than any other building. And should we be surprised if all people in church are not saints? If we think we have problems with public schools, what would America be like without them? As sin and death would much more abound without churches and hospitals, so would ignorance without schools. The public school itself is not *the* problem, and no single solution could significantly reduce learning problems experienced by many children. Problems, like solutions, have many causes.

Part of the Problem—or of the Solution

A hungry, disrespectful, or disruptive child will have difficulty learning in any school with any teacher. An amiable child may, in the course of a single weekend, be turned into a nervous problem learner following the announcement of an impending divorce at home. Evangelicals must be concerned about the subtle slide away from biblical principles in many Christian families. A child's home environment is the single most significant factor in determining how well a child performs in school.

How many Christian parents insist upon a set study time and bedtime? How many send their children off to school fortified with a good breakfast and a good attitude? And how many parents give lip service to academics while reserving their praise for athletic accomplishments? Parents must instill in their children respect for both teachers and scholarship if children are to learn and teachers teach.

Moreover, the endless hours spent addicted to inane television programs negatively affect our children's ability to learn. The typical eighteen-year-old has watched eighteen thousand hours of television, but spent only fifteen thousand hours in school. Talk-show host Phil Donahue once commented that every teacher will have to dress up like Big Bird to get a child's attention. It is difficult to teach under the best of circumstances. It is harder when you are competing with MTV and situation comedies. Television, coupled with a day-care setting, is a poor substitute for involved parenting. What may a teacher realistically expect of a child whose father's undivided attention is available for less than fifteen minutes a day? Back to basics will not stop unsupervised television viewing or help parents become more involved with their children.

And trying to shift our God-appointed parenting responsibilities to a Christian school is not going to solve our children's problems.

Often fundamentalist churches stand back and point an accusatory finger at the public schools. A more productive approach would be to assume part of the responsibility and join with the schools to influence positively the next generation of Americans.

We ought not to leave America. We should not go off into some Christian plantation never to be heard from again. We must not leave the moral destiny of this great nation to others. We must participate.

If public schools are in a crisis, then America is in a crisis. And it will take more than shallow scapegoat reasoning or withdrawing to house or church schools if we are to return to firmer footing. We are in this together. We need public schools. We have either caused our problems or allowed them to evolve unchecked. We must now support, and where needed, reform our schools. We can solve our problems if we assume our personal and collective responsibilities.

Chapter 7, Notes
1. Kenneth L. Tyson, "Schools As Scapegoats," *The School Administrator*, January 1988, 4.

CHAPTER 8

What Do I Need to Know about the Financing of Public Education?

Money collected from taxes is used to support public schools. Three kinds of taxes support American education— property taxes, sales taxes, and income taxes. Property taxes are collected at the local level. Sales tax is a state tax. Income tax can be either a state or a federal tax.

Historically, property tax has been the major source of revenue for local public schools. Property tax is based on the value of real estate and personal property, for example, livestock, automobiles, and stocks. The property tax has been a mainstay for school revenue since the beginnings of public education, when wealth was tied largely to America's agrarian economy.

Tax Reform

In recent years critics have pointed out that the local property tax is an increasingly inadequate and unfair method of raising funds for essential services such as schools and police and fire protection. Poor school districts raise significantly less revenue from property taxes than more affluent districts because the total property value in poorer districts is much lower. Therefore, richer districts can provide better educational opportunities than poorer districts. For example, school districts in the northern suburbs of Chicago, where I taught for many years, can afford to spend more than twice as much per student as nearby Chicago spends. This is true for cities in other areas of the country as well.

In 1973, the Supreme Court acknowledged the need for reform in the system of financing schools.[1] In 1976 the California Supreme Court held that local property tax support for public schools discriminates against children in poor school districts.

The National Education Finance Project conducted research in the early 1970s, reaching several conclusions related to the funding of public education and American values.

1. The opportunity to receive a good education should be equally available to everyone. The level and character of a youngster's education should not depend on the district or state in which he happens to live, or on the wealth of his parents.

2. Education should be seen as helping to break down the barriers of caste and class, providing a path to success for everyone, no matter how humble his birth or circumstance.

3. A government of the people, by the people, and for the people cannot succeed with an illiterate, ignorant citizenry.

4. Systems of taxation should be equitable. People ought to be called upon to support education in proportion to their ability to pay.

5. Education is regarded not just as an expenditure—like buying a ticket to a movie—but as an investment, an investment in human capital, yielding substantial returns to the individual and to society as a whole.[2]

In recent years, the trend has been toward increased state-level support for education. This is helping to equalize the distribution of money to all schools, but it raises the concern that as state governments pay a larger share of school budgets, the state will want to take control of schools away from local districts.

Others resent the fact that poorer districts receive more state and federal money than richer districts. They reason that poorer districts should help themselves. Is the increasing involvement of state government in the funding of public education a positive change, especially in poorer districts?

One of every two black children is born into poverty. One in four lives in inadequate housing and receives inadequate medical attention. Compared with whites, black children are twice as likely to die in infancy. Other poor and uneducated minorities and whites suffer from similar grim statistics.

The cost of human life is overwhelming. Children in the inner city are far more likely than other American children to have only one parent at home; to suffer from birth defects; to have babies while still in their teens; to have low reading scores, high dropout rates, few job skills, and a likelihood of unemployment, crime, and prison.

In Chicago nearly 70 percent of public school students come from families living in poverty. Approximately 40 percent of the public high school students of Chicago will drop out before graduation. In Cleveland, the high school dropout rate actually reaches a numbing 50 percent.

Helping All Americans

Most readers of this book are not inner-city parents. Nevertheless, they should be interested in establishing and maintaining good schools in economically depressed communities. Several passages of Scripture remind us of our personal and collective responsibility to those less fortunate.[3]

It is not just the liberal politician who sees the need to educate poor children. Many hard-nosed capitalists see the dollars-and-cents wisdom of aiding the financially strapped inner-city and rural schools. A few communities have discovered the benefits of "adopt a neighborhood school" programs. These consist of interaction of businesses and communities with their local schools.

Economically, we cannot afford to offer inner-city kids an inadequate education. Educational achievement is tied directly to economic attainment. This is true for children from all income levels. There is also a strong correlation between the single-parent family and child abuse, truancy, substandard school attainment, and high levels of suspensions, unemployment, and juvenile delinquency. Moreover, 75 percent of prison inmates have not finished high school, and 50 percent of these inmates are illiterate.

Head Start is a preschool learning experience for underprivileged three- and four-year-old children. Children learn numbers and words and receive nutritious meals and medical care, all in an effort to help break the cycle of poverty. Does Head Start help? Is it worth the cost?

In 1986, Head Start's twenty-first year, more than 450,000 children were served at an approximate cost of $1 billion. Conservatives and liberals both agree on the value of Head Start. Research showed that needy children who experienced Head Start's early training program were less likely to get into trouble or drop out of school. They were also more likely to go to college and to be employed in good jobs.

One study estimated that Head Start saves seven times its actual cost with fewer people unemployed, fewer people on welfare, and fewer people in prison. And while money is important, it is ultimately the lives of the children that are at stake.

The Ford Foundation identified 202 urban schools that had reversed what were seemingly hopeless educational environments.[4] What did these schools do? What do great schools have in common? *U.S. News and World Report* conducted a study to answer this question. The study discovered that great schools, whether in the inner city or affluent suburbs, possess "a strong principal with clear-cut educational and disciplinary goals, inspired teachers who take an interest in their students' academic and personal problems and parents and local business leaders who are willing to lend a hand."[5]

Financial and emotional support for public schools has been declining in some communities for reasons only indirectly caused by the schools. Years ago, most adults had school-age children or grandchildren and, because of this direct concern, were willing to pay for education in their local community. Education and the accompanying tax dollars were an investment in the future of their own loved ones.

Today fewer than 50 percent of adults have children of school age, and some withdraw their children from public schools to leave society's problems behind and to seek a deeper religious experience.

But problems do not end simply by enrolling in a Christian school. There may be sacrifices and significant problems connected with the Christian school which are just as bad as perceived problems with the public school. What social upheaval will the children experience by the uprooting? Will longer bus rides keep the children away from home additional hours? Many mothers have returned to work to pay for Christian school tuition, only to discover that family life deteriorated during their absence.

We have come a long way since the days of the New England Puritans. Until recent years, almost all churches saw the wisdom of universal public education and supported it. Private school education was viewed as a luxury for affluent citizens.

Churches limited their involvement with private schools primarily to frontier missions and the education of minorities, women, the poor, and handicapped individuals. Today some conservative Christians are withdrawing their children—in addition to their time, talents, and prayers—from the public schools.

Establishing a school presents a local church with a great financial burden. Normal church goals such as missions or other programs requiring financial support become handicapped.

It is my responsibility as a citizen to work for the better use of tax dollars and a better education for all God's children. Can I do this by retreating to a small private Christian school?

Each Christian parent and citizen should feel a sense of obligation and stewardship for the education of the next generation. Usually this is best accomplished by providing support for the local public schools. Each of us believes that children should be provided the best education possible. As adults and parents we have a responsibility to support our schools financially and emotionally and to participate in the education of all of America's children.

Chapter 8, Notes
    1. San Antonio Independent School District v. Rodriguez, 411 U.S. 1 (1973). The court determined that inequities exist but must be corrected through legislative rather than judicial means.
    2. Roe L. Johns, "Toward Equity in School Finance," *American Education*, November 1971, 3-6.
    3. See, for example, Proverbs 14:31; 17:5; 22:9; 31:9; Isaiah 10:1-2; 25:4; Jeremiah 22:16; Amos 2:6-7; 5:11-13, 24; Matthew 19:21; Luke 4:18; 14:13; Acts 10:4; Galatians 2:10; James 2:1- 5.
    4. "What Makes Great Schools Great," *U.S. News and World Report*, 27 August 1984, 46.
    5. Ibid.

CHAPTER 9

Kenneth Gangel's Response to David Smith

How refreshing to read these chapters from the pen of an experienced public school educator! I sense his deep and sincere commitment to what he believes God has called him to do. At no point in the following pages of critique should any reader draw from my remarks even the slightest hint at malicious intent nor an attempt to belittle that commitment. As I have written at the end of Chapter eighteen, "the enemy of the Christian school is not the Federal Government, the State Board of Education, the public system." I concern myself only with the text of Dr. Smith's chapters and its arguments.

First, it's imperative that Dr. Smith, other Christian public school leaders, and readers of this book understand the sincerity and professionalism of educational leaders committed to Christian schools. For example, no serious Christian educator favors nor fights for the so-called "prayer amendment." Neither the absence of prayer nor the absence of anything in public education troubles us; it is the *presence* of a day-by-day systematic inculcation of secular humanism as a philosophy of life.

I find myself in agreement with Dr. Smith on the issue of equal access, and I wonder what Christians in public education can do about the many inequities now currently observable in the system. Of course most Christian school leaders debunk the so-called "conspiracy theory" promoted by some sensationalists among us. Dr. Smith tells us that "teachers collectively tend to be a conservative group within our society." But that does not explain the radical liberalism of the National Education Association which he dismisses in one sentence (p. 23). If the Gallup poll to which he refers is correct, why can't this significant majority of public school teachers deflate the clout of such a frightening and powerful lobby?

I challenge Dr. Smith's suggestion that "only a handful of the sixteen thousand school cooperations in America are 'too far gone' to be successfully changed." His involvement in "dozens" hardly represents solid field research. I suspect that almost every major urban system has crossed the line of redemption in moral and ethical dimensions, if not academic.

At the beginning of Chapter two Dr. Smith deflects the criticism of public education, telling us it comes "from well-meaning parents and citizens in general" and "from books declaring that schools are bad." He fails to treat and answer such well-documented and highly publicized studies as "A Nation at Risk," *The Literacy Hoax*, the research of Paul Vitz as well as the concerns of Secretary Bennett. To be sure, American attitudes toward education have changed dramatically, but one must ask whether the changes in public education have not invoked that barrage of criticism. If Smith is right in suggesting that the primary purpose of public education is literacy, then the failure of the system is obvious to all.

But of far greater concern in Dr. Smith's chapters is his misunderstanding of the Christian school movement. He tells us, for example, that "Christian school students often develop a cloistered mentality" and that "students attending Christian high schools reach the conclusion that parents send them there because they cannot handle the world." What documentation does he offer for such brash statements? The first is based upon what "Pastor Haag told me" and the second tells us what "Doug believes." Smith claims "Christian schools do not give students a realistic world view" and that "Christian school kids do not face influences that their peers face." For these conclusions we do not even have a youth pastor's opinion. One need not give space to such undocumented assertion; readers are referred to chapters which treat each of these items separately. What parents must remember, however, is that Christian children are citizens of a different "country" with a different set of values and standards, and a very different idea of truth. As a professional educator, I happen to believe the children of God deserve something better than pagan public education. When we give our sons and daughters to the secular system we invite the values, standards, and errors of a godless culture to penetrate their spirits.

Disappointingly, Smith quotes "a middle-age couple" who make an argument for public education by saying "if we remove all 'salt' from our public schools we should not complain about what is left." This faulty logic is capable of a multitude of equally ridiculous applications: "If all Christian young people go to the mission field, who will serve as pastors and youth leaders in our churches at home?"; or, "If everyone goes to church on Sunday morning, who will maintain the appropriate public services to keep the society functioning?"

Of course, it's unlikely that all Christians will rush off to the mission field or that too many people will show up in church on Sunday morning; it's even less likely that all Christian children and young people will abandon the public schools. Christian school educators appeal for parents to consider the options honestly and openly, not to abandon the public system in its entirety.

Smith also raises the straw man of sectarian fundamentalism in Christian education. Of course they exist, just as child-molesting homosexuals and mind-bending atheists exist in the public schools. But such a caricature represents a "cheap shot" argument unworthy of this serious work.

By the time we get half-way through Chapter five we understand the problem: Dr. Smith does not understand Christian education. He shows no familiarity with any serious Christian school writer or work at any point in the eight chapters. He appears to be totally unaware of the Association of Christian Schools International, Christian Schools International, the American Association of Christian Schools and any other responsible group promoting Christian school education in America. Without documentation he complains that Christian school advocates blame public schools for national problems; American students perform as well as their counterparts in other industrialized nations; and that Christian education is a "ghettoizing," or isolating of the Christian faith which "our children know is unnatural." Every Christian educator I know is opposed to "ghettoizing" and most work very hard at preventing that problem in their schools.

In chapter six Smith raises his argument a notch when he deals with something he does understand. I seriously doubt that "the majority of Christian parents have made a conscious decision to send their children to the local public school," but in general, Christian school leaders have no problem with Smith's emphasis on strong Christian homes and their role in healthy childhood development.

Chapter eight offers helpful information about the way public schools use tax-generated dollars, information we all need to know. On page 71, however, Smith's rhetoric has deteriorated into threats, warning his readers that parents who opt for the Christian school face "sacrifices and significant problems."

Of greatest concern, however, is Smith's seemingly precarious grasp of the history and philosophy of education. What could he possibly mean by saying that the New England Puritans "saw the development of sectarian schools as both un-American and undemocratic"? With their total conviction to preserve Calvinistic doctrine and a strict separatistic lifestyle, their severe beliefs in total depravity and election, and their absolute commitment to the dominance of the Bible in all of education, early New England schools were the most sectarian this nation has ever seen! Private schools were irrelevant since every public school was a Christian school.

In his conclusion Dr. Smith challenges us "to work for the better use of tax dollars and a better education for all of God's children" and wonders whether we can do that by "retreating to a small private Christian school." In my opinion, the more pressing responsibility is my role as a parent to protect and nurture the spiritual sensitivity of my children so that their formal schooling complements the instruction of their parents and their church. With this priority the crucial question becomes, "Can I do this when depending on a large public secular school?"

CHAPTER 10

Gregg Harris's Response to David Smith

THERE is no doubt in my mind that Dr. Smith is a true missionary to the public school system. He is obviously dedicated to serving Christ and to reaching all children with the gospel. He and others like him have done their best to make an intolerable situation better. But better is just not good enough for parents who are seeking to prepare their children for life.

What may often begin as a reaction to what is wrong with the public schools quickly turns to excitement about what is right about the home. Home-school parents are rediscovering the joy and delight of personal study. They want to instill in their children the skills needed to continue to learn anything they will ever need to know.

Dr. Smith's argument that it is much easier to provide excellent education if you are only going to educate relatively few children is really an argument in favor of the home school. He also says that private schools maintain a better statistical average than public schools because they have greater selectivity. It is true that public schools are required to accept any student regardless of the level of his ability, and that fact does drag down their statistical averages. Yet the home school accepts any student that comes to it by birth or by adoption, and in spite of this "take-whatever-comes" policy, the home schools, statistical averages are still usually better than those of the public schools.[1]

Dr. Smith closes his section on the educational advantages of public schools by stating that for the majority of children, the public schools offer the best teaching techniques, the best curriculum, the best extracurricular opportunities, and generally the best overall and comprehensive education available (chapter four). He may have documentation for these statements, but I haven't seen it. These generalizations and unsupported statements sound like wishful thinking.

A number of recent studies demonstrate that home school children are receiving a comparable if not above average education, and the level of the parents' education or issues of certification, in general, does not seem to affect the educational achievement of their children.[2]

Concerning the social benefits for Christian students in the public schools, Dr. Smith states that it is virtually impossible to isolate ourselves and our children completely from evil people. That is true. And anyone who would want to do so is abandoning the Great Commission. That is not our intention. To the contrary, our goal has always been to give our children a better start in life so that they will be prepared to deal with the confrontations and the contacts they will inevitably have in this world.

Dr. Smith writes that it is time to end the type of Christian faith that is impotent and relegated solely to the private places of home and church. I agree. But faith must at least start there. He rightly rejects the kind of faith that is expected to have no influence on how we think or act—at school, at work, or at any societal function—yet I have seen firsthand how quickly the environment of the public school can smother godly zeal. It encourages Christians, teachers and students alike, to imagine they are having a "quiet impact" and to rationalize that someday the fruit will be more visible. In reality they are unopposed by the ungodly merely because they are doing the secularists no harm. The administration may even use the shy Christian teacher as evidence of school's religious tolerance.

In any discussion of social influence, it is necessary to be specific about who we expect to influence whom. Home school parents know that high school level students can have a tremendous impact on a public school. I know of some former home school students who are founding Bible clubs on public school campuses today. Junior high students tend to have less confidence. Elementary level students are more often influenced than influential.

Dr. Smith may have a few examples of a younger child being a blessing to his public school classmates, but for every "blessing" I can document a traumatic disaster. Pecking orders, bullies, peer orientation, and social rejection are painful and predictable. Home school parents are not hiding their children from the "real" world or the "relevant" world. We simply have a sense of the seasons of a child's readiness to face various aspects of the world.

Dr. Smith says that many parents are isolating their children in opposition to principles set forth in the Bible. He fails, however, to state exactly what those principles are. While acknowledging that the Scriptures give parents the responsibility of child-training, he introduces the public schools as some kind of friendly reinforcement. He acknowledges that a good Christian home is the most important influence in a child's life. However, Dr. Beauvais at the University of Colorado has found that this influence is quickly lost; a child's friends in school wield five times more influence over his decision to abuse drugs than any other lifestyle factor.

Dr. Smith repeatedly makes the mistake of referring to the neighborhood public schools as an experience of reality. As I will argue later, the real world is not an age-segregated world. The real world is not at all like school. The idea that children need to go into an artificially-contrived setting in order to experience reality is absurd. The school is Dr. Smith's real world because he works there.

Dr. Smith states that the responsibility of public school educators is to teach and model the important character traits and national values about which our society agrees. Public schools, he says, should not concentrate upon deeply-held convictions which divide us as Americans. But such a view robs the Christian of the high ground in teaching the world proper biblical values and ideas. Many important issues today divide us, and our nation resolves conflict by allowing all voices to have their hearing in the market place, including the Christian voice. Public schools seek to create the illusion that Christianity should make peace or come to some kind of truce with the unbelieving world. This is not the case. To do so is apostasy.

We are dealing with a period in history when it is important that those who have strong convictions state those convictions in clear and unequivocal terms. As Christians, we cannot afford to minimize such sins as abortion, lust, homosexuality, or greed, nor should we stand still when these issues are "up for grabs" in public school classes.

Dr. Smith has an unflagging confidence in the school's faithfulness to its original purpose to contribute to national unity. He states that our schools have helped support basic traditional values. In looking at the generations I see coming out of the public schools, the question is, "Where are those traditional values?" How is it that the National Education Association can openly support abortion, gay liberation, and feminism and, at the same time, be supporting basic traditional values? The public schools are extremely liberal.

The public schools like to take responsibility for the upward mobility of our nation when, in fact, the abundance that we enjoyed before the world wars was a result of the agrarian character of the average family and the industrialization of our urban communities. Since the world wars, our prosperity has been the result of being virtually untouched by the wars. Our factories were not bombed; our houses were not destroyed. Although we lost many lives in those conflicts, our means of production continued unaffected. To place our prosperity at the door of the public school is misdirected. This is especially so in view of the federal government's own negative evaluation of public education entitled "A Nation at Risk." Our nation is as strong as it is today in spite of the public schools.

At the same time public school educators wish to take responsibility for the positive occurrences in our society, they want to reject responsibility for the negative trends. When confronted with the questions of drug abuse, they prefer to blame parents. Never mind that these children do not get their first exposure to drug abuse at home. When confronted with the high illiteracy rate, they again prefer to blame parents for not enriching the preschooler's experience. But parents have been wooed into abdicating their responsibilities by the promises of the public schools. When asked to consider having competency tests administered to public school teachers, the National Education Association cries out that this would be unfair. Is it fair to accept more and more money while showing fewer and fewer results and being less and less accountable?

The question of how the individual Christian family should respond to the plight of the public schools and their funding is best explained in terms of good neighbor-liness. A neighbor should take care of his own yard first. He should do all that is necessary to be sure that his share of the neighborhood is neat and clean and safe. If everyone would only sweep the street in front of his own house, the entire street would be clean. That is what home schoolers are doing in the educational neighbor-hood.

I believe the best thing the Christian family can do for its community is to assure that its own children get the best possible education available. Christian parents are able to do far more than this however. Based on their understanding of the needs of their community and the political implications that are placed before them, home schooling families are responding. If the Christian family believes that the local public schools are sound and that they have integrity, they support them with their tax dollars by voting in support of levies and sales taxes.

However, when the local school proves to be insen-sitive to the interests of parents and unwilling to change bad school policy, parents should express their dissatisfac-tion by voting down school levies. For all the rhetoric used by the schools to explain why it is so necessary to have additional funds, it amazes me that their solution to nearly every school problem is to have longer hours and more teachers, the predictable response of any union faced with a major contract negotiation. And when they are forced to make budget cuts the first things they cut are basic services. They leave their pet projects and birth control clinics intact and do away with whatever is most likely to make the taxpayers squeal "uncle." Parents have had it with these tactics. The attendance at my Home Schooling Workshop always rises in an area just following a teacher's strike. Some parents are saying, "Keep your petty strikes. We are teaching our children at home."

In evaluating each of the options set forth in this book, parents should ask three basic questions: *First*, where will my children receive the best education? By this I do not mean merely acquiring skills in reading, writing, and arithmetic. Where will they acquire these ideas from God's perspective? *Second*, whose values do I want my children to emulate? And *third*, am I really ready to part with my child during the precious early years of his education? Is your child ready to part from you?

I believe the home schooling option is a better alternative than public schools for providing satisfactory answers to these critical questions.

Chapter 10, Notes
1. Jon Wartes, "Washington Homeschool Research Project Report from the 1987 Washington Homeschool Testing" (Woodinville, Washington, 1988).
2. Jennie Finlayson Rakestraw, "An Analysis of Home Schooling for Elementary School-Age Children in Alabama" (diss., University of Alabama, 1987). See especially pp. 125-40 for conclusions and summary of controlled studies between home schooled children and public school children.

PART 2

CHRISTIAN SCHOOL EDUCATION

Kenneth Gangel

CHAPTER 11

Is There a Biblical Basis for Christian Schools?

EDUCATION has always been foundational to the spread of the Christian message. Christianity finds its source of truth in a book, the Bible. The Bible reveals that the people of God have always been concerned with education, because God's communication to us and our communication to others depends on it. Christian education finds its impetus in this biblical emphasis on education. Especially is this important with the education of our children.

Biblical Reasons for Christian Schools

Each month Paul Kienel writes a one-page article for *Christian School Comment*, a publication of the Association of Christian Schools International. Occasionally he asks a guest author to contribute, and on one occasion that guest was Dr. Wayne Grudem, Associate Professor of New Testament at Trinity Evangelical Divinity School, Deerfield, Illinois. His article entitled "Biblical Reasons for Sending Children to a Christian School" is used here with permission.

The main reason my wife Margaret and I sent our children to our local Christian school was a conviction that Scripture directs Christian parents to give their children a Bible-based education whenever they have opportunity to do so. I have listed here six biblical principles which we found very persuasive.

1. All of a child's education should be Bible-centered and God-centered.

"Parents, do not exasperate your children; instead, bring them up in the training and instruction of the Lord" (Ephesians 6:4).

I'm saddened when Christian parents tell me of the frustration and stress their children experience in secular schools, but I also wonder if parents aren't doing exactly what Ephesians 6:4 says not to do: putting their children, day after day, in situations that "exasperate" them, that "provoke them to anger," sorrow or frustration.

Training that is not "of the Lord" will do that: the contrast in the verse ("do not exasperate . . . instead bring them up in the training of the Lord") tells us we should expect "exasperated" children from secular education.

2. Education should be positive and truthful.

Sometimes parents think that a secular environment will "strengthen" their children by forcing them to stand up for their own beliefs. But God's Word does not endorse that viewpoint. It does not say, "give a child twelve years of training in the way he should not go, and he will be made strong by it." Instead, God tells us,

"Train a child in the way he should go, and when he is old he will not turn from it" (Proverbs 22:6).

I know of no verse of Scripture that tells me that secular training will "strengthen" Christian children. It may *callous* them so they view sin as more "normal." It may *harden* them so they care more about the things of the world and less about God.

It may *desensitize* them so they are more comfortable living in the midst of repeated sin against their Lord. But it will not *strengthen* them as Christian men and women: "Train a child in the way he *should* go."

3. Peer influence should be positive and Christ-like.

Parents sometimes think it helps or strengthens their children to spend much time with children who have different moral standards and goals for life. But God's Word disagrees and reminds us that children will tend to become more and more like their frequent companions:

"He who walks with the wise grows wise, but a companion of fools suffers harm" (Proverbs 13:20).

"Do not be deceived, 'Bad company ruins good morals'" (1 Corinthians 15:33).

This year we've seen the results of good peer influence in our boys' lives. They've picked up from friends at our Christian Academy a deeper concern for prayer, for purity of speech, for missions, for kindness to others, for respect for authority, etc. And in general they're happier! They love their school. Their education is the kind God wants it to be—and even very young children sense that, although they can't explain it.

4. Every teacher's pattern of life should be worthy of imitation.

Children are great imitators. A teacher they like will have tremendous impact not only on studies, but on attitudes toward all aspects of life. Jesus knew that, for He said,

"Every one when he is fully taught will be like his teacher" (Luke 6:40).

5. Only God-centered education gives true wisdom.

"The fear of the LORD is the beginning of wisdom" (Psalm 111:10).

"The fear of the LORD is the beginning of knowledge" (Proverbs 9:10).

"In Christ are hidden all the treasures of wisdom and knowledge" (Colossians 2:3).

This is the reason our secular educational systems have strayed from the truth. Isn't it foolish to think we can get a true perspective on God's creation from a system that begins by excluding His words?

Here is the issue: Do we really think the Bible works in the real world? That it gives critical guidance in modern life? If not—if we quietly assume the Bible is mainly intended for use inside Sunday school classes—then secular education will be our natural choice. But if we do think the Bible guides us in all areas of life, then we'll give our children education that applies Scripture to every area of training for life.

6. Christian schooling is the best hope for transforming society.

Jesus tells us, "You are the salt of the earth . . . you are the light of the world" (Matthew 5:13, 14).

Society is to be influenced and guided by Christians! But why aren't we doing this more today?

I think the largest reason is our meek acceptance of secular education all the way from kindergarten to the university doctorate.

School is where we learn to *think*. It's where we learn how to *work* and *relate to others* and *influence the world*. But if that whole process excludes God's own viewpoint in Scripture, for twelve years our Christian witness grows accustomed to being mute, and it remains *un*educated, never growing beyond the "Sunday school" level. Our lamp is "put under a bushel," and our salt loses its saltiness and is "no longer good for anything" (Matthew 5:13, 15).

Christian parents sometimes say they want their children to be "salt and light" in secular schools. But how much salt and light can *untrained, silent* Christians be?

Must we not rather train our children in Christian

schools that they may become tasty salt and brilliant lights to transform a society wandering in darkness?

The Central Premise of Christian Education

Professor Grudem's article provides an important biblical statement about Christian school education. The purpose of Christian schools is to present to our children, as clearly as possible, the truth about God, about life, about our world and everything in it, and to present the Word of God as the authoritative source upon which to build a life that has purpose and meaning.

Christian education designs to train the thinking patterns of its students. Those young minds must be developed because thinking Christians are called upon to construct an evangelical world and life view. According to James Sire, "A world view is a set of presuppositions or assumptions which we hold (consciously or unconsciously) about the basic make-up of the world."[1] It is essential, therefore, for every Christian to learn how to interpret his culture "Christianly." To perform this requires an analysis of society enlightened by God's revelation. At the center of that exercise is a clear-cut knowledge of the Word of God.

Since there is a God, and since God has spoken in history, the most important aspect of learning for the Christian is to find out what God has said. God's revelation, both special and natural, becomes the heart and core of the curriculum in any Christian institution at any level. That position stands against rationalism, the view that man alone is responsible for the creation and certification of truth.

Let us remember too that the kind of faith the Bible demands is no mindless commodity. Far from asking students to abandon mental faculties and intellectual integrity, the quality Christian school seeks to develop students' minds as a significant part of the holistic person.

Christian theism stands in opposition to secular atheism. The foundational construct for education centers in an understanding of ultimate reality which, for the Christian, begins with the very earliest words of Scripture—"In the beginning, God."

The first and most significant tool of the Christian teacher, therefore, is Scripture, which is the first and final textbook of the Christian school. I do not wish to argue the old cliche that the Bible is not a specific textbook of biology, politics, or any other discipline beyond theology. The cliche is basically true; nevertheless, the Bible was the primary textbook in early American schools.

The Role of the Bible in Christian Education

We are not just talking about *knowledge* of the Bible. Essential for the achievement of truth transmission in the Christian classroom is a commitment to the *authority* of the Bible. That great pioneer of the modern Christian education movement, Dr. Frank E. Gaebelein, once identified four reasons the Word of God must be central in Christian education.

1. The sheer, unapproachable greatness of the written Word of God; to take as the center of the curriculum the one book among all the other great books to which alone the superlative "greatest" can without challenge be uniquely applied—this is neither narrow nor naive. Rather it is simply good judgment to center on the best rather than the second best.

2. Its authority as the inspired, inerrant Word of God.

3. Its indispensable critical function. In a day of debased values and satisfaction with the second and even third rate, education requires a standard and point of reference by which the cheapened standards of our day may be judged.

4. It relates to the all important matter of knowing and finding the truth.[2]

The integration of truth, at least the way I use the term, refers to the teaching of all subjects as a part of the total truth of God, thereby enabling the student to see the unity of natural and special revelation. Such integration requires that Bible-centered education extend to all areas of student life. Just as there is no divorce of the sacred and the secular in the genuinely Christian life, so there is no divorce between faith and learning (nor between faith and any other activity) on the distinctively Christian campus. A student able to memorize Bible verses for personal evangelism or offer a profound explanation of the Westminster Shorter Catechism is not a positive product of the system unless that knowledge affects his life in the hallways, on the football field, and in relations with his family at home.

The Christian school which speaks openly of its integration of faith and learning has the accompanying responsibility of demonstrating how that posture is implemented in the lives of students at all times and all places. Biblical Christian education is holistic ministry.

Dr. Norman Harper has written an extremely helpful book describing Christian school education. In it he emphasizes the very centrality of Christ in such schools.

> A Christian school is a Christian academic community with the distinctive task of equipping students individually and corporately to exercise dominion in Christ over all that He has made.... No individual can do everything, but the child of God can be taught to bring himself and all that has been entrusted to him into subjection to the Lord Jesus Christ.[3]

The Word of God in the flesh—Jesus—and the Word of God in written form—the Bible—are the two balancing ingredients of biblical Christian schools.

Chapter 11, Notes
1. James Sire, *The Universe Next Door* (Downers Grove, Ill.: InterVarsity Press, 1976), 17.
2. Frank E. Gaebelein, *A Varied Harvest* (Grand Rapids, Mich.: Wm. B. Eerdmans Publishing Co., 1967), 42-44.
3. Norman E. Harper, *Making Disciples* (Jackson, Miss.: Christian Studies Center, 1981), 68-69.

CHAPTER 12

How Did Christian School Education Begin?

"Education," says Oswald Chambers, "is a bringing out of what is there and giving it the power of expression, not packing in what does not belong; and spiritual education means learning how to give expression to the Divine life that is in us when we are born from above."[1]

Those who teach and administer in Christian schools are servants of God ministering to the next generation. The Christian school is really an extension of the home and the church (in that order), and therefore participates in the general purpose of making students more Christlike. An ideal toward which Christian school educators constantly aim appears in Paul's magnificent words to the Philippians: "Finally, brothers, whatever is true, whatever is noble, whatever is right, whatever is pure, whatever is lovely, whatever is admirable—if anything is excellent or praiseworthy—think about such things" (4:8).

The purpose of Christian school education is to expose students to the real world as revealed through the eyes of God and to instill solid defenses against conformity to the unreal world of the secular community. Scripture says, "Do not conform any longer to the pattern of this world" (Romans 12:2). We are to be in conformity with God, not the secular world which we believe is out of touch with God's reality. As Francis Schaeffer has said, "the final reality is a living and personal God."[2] Christian school educators are committed to inspiring children to become followers of Jesus Christ.

Parental Control

Christian educators believe that children are gifts of God and that parents are responsible for their education and training.

> Hear, O Israel: The LORD our God, the LORD is one. Love the LORD your God with all your heart and with all your soul and with all your strength. These commandments that I give you today are to be upon your hearts. Impress them on your children. Talk about them when you sit at home and when you walk along the road, when you lie down and when you get up. Tie them as symbols on your hands and bind them on your foreheads. Write them on the doorframes of your houses and on your gates (Deuteronomy 6:4-9).

These biblical commands are not directed to the state or federal government or even to the church, but rather the parents to whom children really belong. The government and the church can and should be supportive of parents in their responsibility to carry out their God-given mission as the primary educators of their children. Families, churches, schools, and even friends ought to function in a way which aids parents to train each child "in the way he should go."

Since an overwhelming percentage of any child's time is spent in school or school-related activities (approximately 40-50 percent of his waking hours during the weeks when school is in session), parents must be particularly sensitive to the kind of learning environment surrounding their children.

From the Christian school point of view, the priority of the home is crucial. The school must become its partner in building families rather than test scores or athletic teams. Parental voice in Christian school education is crucial to the very understanding of the term.

Christian Nurture

Christian school educators believe that what children are taught in school should be a direct extension of Christian parents' views. Some Christian schools include evangelism as part of their overall objectives, while others focus on the development of the student who already professes a relationship with Christ. Perhaps the overall biblical objective is spelled out most clearly in Colossians 1:28 and 29: "We proclaim him, admonishing and teaching everyone with all wisdom, so that we may present everyone perfect in Christ. To this end I labor, struggling with all his energy, which so powerfully works in me."

The teachers who teach our children should be the kind of teachers you would personally hire if you had the opportunity to select them. Their lifestyles should directly extend the lifestyle that you and your spouse lead before your children. Their spiritual and social standards should be in harmony with yours.

Do you know the views held by your children's teachers on such subjects as homosexuality, evolution, situation ethics, and other social issues? Students tend to follow the lifestyle and philosophical patterns of their teachers. This is borne out in Scripture. "A student is not above his teacher, but everyone who is fully trained will be like his teacher" (Luke 6:40). Why is it that many parents care deeply who teaches their children in Sunday school, but Monday through Friday glibly place their precious children under teachers whose lifestyles and philosophies directly contradict everything for which those parents stand?

It is interesting that many public school teachers choose Christian schools for their own children. According to *Harper's Index,* 38 percent of Chicago's public school teachers send their children to private schools; but of course, those are not all Christian schools. In another survey conducted by Dr. Paul Kienel of the Association of Christian Schools International (ACSI), several public school teachers responded by offering their reasons for such a choice.

> Public schools assume that man is the product of evolution and most teachers accept this as established. Therefore the basic foundations of morality are based on temporary expediency. The Christian school teaches and exemplifies morality based on unchanging truth. The attitude toward the student sharply contrasts.
>
> The public school teacher too often looks at the student as a number, the ministry of teaching as a job. Most teachers in the Christian school try to understand the uniqueness of each student. As a consequence of the above, most graduates of Christian schools are better prepared intellectually and morally to face the problems of adult life.
>
> The social and academic climate of the public junior high school failed to inspire confidence in my wife and me. The "anything goes" culture, with its loose and conflicting standards and indefinite guidelines would have left our children confused and uncertain regarding life's values. Our Christian school provides a consistent climate for growth and learning through clearly defined guidelines for values based on the unchanging truths of God's Word. The peace of mind shared with us by our children that their well-being in all its forms is the chief concern of

our school is worth many times more than the cost
of tuition.

We send our children to a Christian school to supplement the basic principles they are taught at home
in real-life situations. We also appreciate the fact
that wholesome activities are provided for them,
and their closest friends are Christians.[3]

The U. S. Department of Education commissioned
a Washington think tank to analyze detailed Census Bureau data covering 5 percent of the population in thirteen
states. In Albuquerque, New Mexico, it found that private
schools enroll 14 percent of all children but 30 percent
of public school teachers' children; in Atlanta, the figures
are 14 percent and 25 percent; in Denver, 13 percent
and 22 percent; in Memphis, 21 percent and 36 percent;
in New Orleans, 34 percent and 44 percent; and
Washington, D.C., 18 percent and 33 percent.[4]

According to authors Dennis Doyle and Terry
Hartle, the study suggests that a higher percentage of
those who know the public schools best (its teachers) have
less confidence in the public schools than does the public
at large. "When public school teachers send their children
to private schools, it says something about the schools
they teach in," said the authors.[5] One is reminded of the
restaurant whose chefs have chosen to eat somewhere
else.

Some have suggested that there is a new wind blow-
ing in American education. Perhaps the nation is headed
toward an educational pluralism never before experienced. More than two hundred years before state-
controlled public schools came into existence, educational needs were served exclusively by a complex but
workable evangelical Christian school program. When
the public schools came on the scene the pendulum
swung in the other direction. The Christian schools all
but disappeared; the government's public system has

dominated the scene ever since. Now, possibly, we are moving toward a reasonable coexistence.

Truth Transmission

The difference between Christian and secular education involves defining truth. To the secularist, truth is relative and natural; it is to be taught to basically "good" minds. To the Christian, however, truth is absolute and supernatural and taught to minds affected by original sin.

As an educator, I would be the first to affirm that education has done much to raise the quality of life in America; but as a Christian educator, I qualify that statement by insisting that education is not redemptive in and of itself. Over and over again, history has proven that education can so easily be overrated. If education could redeem a society, the Greeks, the Romans, or the Germans had hundreds of years to demonstrate that feat. Yet the past testifies to the ruin of man and his social institutions unless the God of creation intervenes.

In *Distilled Wisdom,* Ramsey MacDonald claims, "A man is not educated who does not know the basic truths of the Bible. . . . The educated man is a man with certain spiritual qualities which make him calm in adversity, happy when alone, just in his dealings, rational and sane in the fullest meaning of that word in all the affairs of life."

The Word of God is absolute truth. The God of the Bible never changes, nor does His truth vary from one day to the next. It never becomes outdated; it is not in need of constant reworking. Christian education emphasizes absolute truth based on eternal values. The two systems (public and Christian) stand in genuine disharmony; the issue of God's revelation divides Christians and non-Christians right at the beginning of all educational discussions (2 Timothy 3:14-17).

Historical Perspective

On October 31, 1517, a young Augustinian monk by the name of Martin Luther burst on the religious scene of Europe by nailing his ninety-five theses to the door of the castle church at Wittenberg, Germany. Most Christians know Luther as a reformer, a pastor, and a prolific writer. But he was also one of the first educators in history who emphasized the need for universal compulsory education, mainly because he was so concerned that every citizen be able to read the Bible. But the schools he advocated were distinctly Christian, rigidly rejecting both the secularism and the clericalism of his day.

John Calvin, a Swiss contemporary of Luther, also saw the need for Christian schools. He founded Geneva Academy in 1559 and established schools in other cities as well. To ensure compulsory attendance, Luther placed his Christian schools under the auspices of the German civil authorities. Calvin, on the other hand, believed that education was a ministry of the church.

Calvin's ideas of religious liberty and Bible-centered education were carried to the New World by the Pilgrims and Puritans. As in the Christian schools of Luther and Calvin in Europe, attendance in colonial schools was required by civil law, and taxes were raised to support them. But tuition was also required for early Christian schools.

While the approach to learning and the subjects taught were decidedly different from today's Christian schools, numerous parallels exist between America's early schools and the modern Christian school movement. For example, the spiritual and academic quality of colonial schools was a reaction to the depraved educational situation in England. John Winthrop wrote, "The fountains of learning and religion are so corrupted [in England] most children, even the best wits . . . are perverted, corrupted and utterly overthrown by the multitude of evil examples."[6] Small wonder the colonists were committed to quality Christian education which served the country well from 1620 to 1837, a span of 217 years.

Slowly, however, the spiritual rebellion that brought about the rise of Unitarianism also created a climate for state-supported public schools. In addition to the theological fall of Harvard, the increasingly popular teaching of German pantheism, and a gradual spiritual decline of Congregationalism, church and state cleavage was intensified on April 20, 1837, when the Massachusetts legislature established a state board of education composed of eight members who were empowered to appoint their own state secretary of education. Two months later, this first state board of education appointed Unitarian Horace Mann, president of the Massachusetts State Senate, as its new Secretary of Education. He vigorously pursued his responsibilities. Understandably, Horace Mann was regarded as the father of public education, an education that was "centralized, state-controlled . . . governed by a state bureaucracy and financed by taxes on property."[7]

The original consensus that God held authority over both church and state began to fade. The transition was slow, but the state started marching to a man-centered, humanistic drummer. Liberal-thinking legislators accepted the German Hegelian idea that man's laws are superior to God's laws.

But that was New England. In the nineteenth century the Ohio frontier produced a man who gave public education significant credibility in Protestant America: education reformer and Presbyterian minister William Holmes McGuffey. McGuffey's *Eclectic Readers* were studied by 80 percent of America's students.[8] Between 1836 and 1920, 120 million copies of McGuffey's *Readers* were sold. Only the Bible and Webster's Dictionary were more popular.

Since 1837, various groups have used public education for a variety of reasons. Horace Mann and the Harvard Unitarians used public education to weaken the long-established compatibility of the church and state and to introduce America to a secular, non-Biblical form of instruction. William McGuffey and the Protestant community used public education to advance conservative Protestantism.

Enter John Dewey, a philosophy professor at Columbia University in New York, who used the nation's public schools to advance secular humanism. An avowed atheist, Dewey was the first president of the American Humanist Association and the principal author of Humanist Manifesto I in 1933.[9]

> In 1859 a mantle was transferred in New England. Horace Mann died in Massachusetts, and John Dewey was born in Vermont. It is very possible that those two men have been the most influential educational leaders in America from the day the Pilgrims first rode ashore to the present hour.[10]

During the early years of this century, Dewey's school of education at Columbia became the philosophical touchstone for all government-funded state colleges and other teacher-training institutions across America. The impact of his "progressive education" ideas divested America's public schools of their Christian character and made them insensitive to the evangelical community. His man-centered idea that children are perfectible through faith in man, not faith in God, was an act of defiance against God. The moral and academic devastation that followed has handicapped the lives of millions of Americans.

By the time Dewey died in 1952, the overpoweringly Protestant character of the early public schools was barely visible. Eventually, however, conservative evangelical Protestants began the long trek back to re-establishing Protestant, Bible-centered elementary and secondary schools for their children. The re-establishment of Christian schools was slow at first, but as government-funded public schools became increasingly insensitive to the evangelical community, there was a dramatic increase in the number of Christian schools. A survey of the founding dates among the elementary and secondary schools in the 1986 ACSI Directory is instructive.[11]

Christian schools founded through 1950   82
Christian schools founded between 1951 and 1960   99
Christian schools founded between 1961 and 1970   173
Christian schools founded between 1971 and 1980   827
Christian schools founded between 1981 and 1986   714
(6-year period)

In a sense, the nation has come full circle in education. American education from the Plymouth colony school in 1620 up until the beginning of secular public education in 1837 was totally Christian in character. However, we have come a long way from the Plymouth colony. In *The Evolution of American Secondary School Texts,* Paul Vitz reports that before 1776, religion and morals accounted for over 90 percent of schools' readers. By 1926, this number was down to 6 percent, and in more recent times, it has been too small to be measured.

When evangelical Christians realized that public schools were no longer philosophically compatible with biblical values, they began to re-establish evangelical schools. The vast majority of evangelical Christians, though, are still not in stride with the burgeoning Christian school movement. Only a small portion of today's Christian community provides the Bible-centered form of education prevalent during the first 217 years of America's history. Currently, twenty thousand to twenty-five thousand evangelical Protestant Christian schools serve the fifty states. If given the freedom to flourish, Christian schools could make a significant difference in the moral and academic character of our country.

Chapter 12, Notes
    1. Oswald Chambers, "The Place of Help," *Christianity Today*, 4 April 1986, 55.
    2. Francis A. Schaeffer, from a speech delivered at an ACSI teacher's convention in Anaheim, Calif., 1983.
    3. A public high school teacher whose children attend Wescove Christian High School in Potomac, Ill.; reported by Paul Kienel.
    4. Reported by Paul Kienel, ACSI.
    5. *The Daily Review*, 17 March 1986, 11.
    6. The spirit of preserving "doctrinal purity" was paramount in the thinking of the Calvinistic Congregationalist Puritans from England as they settled around Boston Harbor in the early 1600s. Governor John Winthrop of the Massachusetts Bay Colony wrote that colonial schools were "for the zealous purification of the church and commonwealth." Lawrence Cremin, *American Education: The Colonial Experience, 1607-1783* (New York: Harper & Row, 1970).
    7. Samuel L. Blumenfeld, *Is Public Education Necessary* (Old Greenwich, Conn.: The Devin-Adair Co., 1981), 184.
    8. In *McGuffey and His Readers*, John H. Westerhoff III notes: "The Northwest Ordinance of 1787 stated that 'religion, morality and knowledge are necessary to good government and the happiness of mankind.' McGuffey's Readers supported that contention and provided a resource for the education of Christians. First religion, then morality, and last, knowledge—that was the focus of their content.

"We should not be surprised, therefore, to learn that McGuffey's Readers read more like a theology textbook than a children's elementary schoolbook. Life is God-conscious and God-centered in McGuffey's Readers." John H. Westerhoff III, *McGuffey and His Readers* (Milford, Mich.: Mott Media, 1978), 103.
    9. Paul Kurtz, ed., *Humanist Manifesto I and II* (Buffalo, N.Y.: Prometheus Books, 1973), 11.
    10. Kenneth O. Gangel and Warren S. Benson, *Christian Education: Its History and Philosophy* (Chicago: Moody Press, 1983), 291.
    11. ACSI Directory, 1987.

CHAPTER 13

What Are the Spiritual Advantages of a Christian School Education?

THE apostle Paul said, "Do not conform any longer to the pattern of this world, but be transformed by the renewing of your mind" (Romans 12:2). Yet Christian young people who attend non-Christian schools are being adjusted to the world; they are being conformed to it. Paul further states, "Everyone has heard about your obedience, so I am full of joy over you; but I want you to be wise about what is good, and innocent about what is evil" (Romans 16:19). These verses hardly support that idea that we should expose our children to an anti-faith environment.

Some Christian school leaders believe that representatives of the public school community are becoming increasingly bold in their intolerance of Christian convictions. Attorneys representing the Hawkins County (Tennessee) School Board in the Mozert textbook trial said,

"It is impossible to accommodate people with these kinds of religious beliefs in the public schools." The case centers around seven Christian families who objected to a public school curriculum that requires students to read stories which suggest that "lying is acceptable, stealing is permissible and . . . trains children how to concoct occult chants or incantations."[1]

The Christian school contains many imperfections; it is not heaven on earth. The question, however, is not perfection. Rather, we must ask what God would have us provide for our children in the present secular world where He and His Word are not welcome. As this book explains, there are really only three options from which the parent can choose. The real question is which is the most biblical?

Education for Righteousness

Theodore Roosevelt frequently said, "To educate a child in mind and not in morals is to educate a menace to society." Education must contain more than cold academics. True education trains children how to live—not just how to make a living. Life consists of more than making money, acquiring possessions, and pursuing pleasures. A popular bumper sticker misleads to the point of danger: "He who dies with the most toys wins."

True education trains children how to be happy in life without committing sin. Christian school educators teach children that God's program of happiness supersedes the world's program of pleasure. Consider these phrases from the Bible:

"blessed is he who trusts in the LORD" (Proverbs 16:20).

"blessed are the people whose God is the LORD" (Psalm 144:15).

"for the joy of the LORD is your strength" (Nehemiah 8:10).

"with eternal pleasures at your right hand" (Psalm 16:11).

These passages speak of an eternal happiness, joy, and pleasure which are different from the temporary "pleasures of sin for a short time" (Hebrews 11:25) so typical of the world. The born-again child is a new creature in Christ—totally "re-programmed." Old things have passed away. Everything becomes brand new (2 Corinthians 5:17). He has a new Director and a new direction. Instead of pleasing himself, he now lives to please the Lord.

Christian schools attempt to inspire youngsters to Christian servanthood rather than pleasure-seeking, self-centered living. The Greeks called the pursuit of pleasure "hedonism." Its followers set their highest ambitions on self-pleasure. In Christian school education, we attempt to train students to keep Christ at the center of their lives and to use the Bible to discern between the ways of the world and the ways of God.

Education for Morality

A recent magazine advertisement with a near-nude couple partially submerged in a lagoon carried in large type a single word: hedonism. In small type below were these words: "On a sugar white beach in Jamaica, there's a secluded spot where you can forget about money, schedules, and give yourself up to the total pursuit of pleasure known as hedonism." Then the ad listed a series of hedonistic pleasures such as "wine, parties and beautiful people from everywhere." To those whose god is sensual pleasure, the ad has strong appeal.

Perhaps you are saying, "Christian schools must be made up of grim souls who cannot possibly enjoy life." To the contrary, in Christian education we teach young people that life in Christ is exciting. They can thoroughly enjoy living and at the same time maintain a godly perspective on life. Consider the following biblical principles:

- Do not participate in sinful pleasures that violate the Word of God. "If sinners entice you, do not give in to them" (Proverbs 1:10).
- Do not allow the pursuit of pleasure to become the main preoccupation of your life. Your highest ambition should be to do the will of God. "I desire to do your will, O my God" (Psalm 40:8).
- Do not center your life in service to self; "be a good minister of Christ Jesus, brought up in the truths of the faith and of the good teaching that you have followed" (1 Timothy 4:6).

Negative advice? No! The pursuit of wanton pleasure and self-centered living leads to a meaningless life. All of us need moral direction for our lives, an immovable standard for moral excellence which can be found only in God's Word.

Education for Truth

Dewey, like his philosophic mentor, Hegel, believed that children should be taught they need not follow a fixed standard of right and wrong, that no such standard exists. Dewey, Hegel, Rousseau, and others advocated the erroneous idea that man has no obligation to "God" and that even young children should create their own standards of right and wrong. Sound familiar? In the twelfth century B.C., Scripture tells us that "everyone did as he saw fit" (Judges 17:6). American public education, in general, stands committed to the ideologies of man—not God's Word; it ultimately depicts a secular paganism.

In their book *What Are They Teaching Our Children?*, Mel and Norma Gabler include this interesting "parable" about children in public schools:

Imagine that 50 young children are picked up from their homes and bused to a marina. Each will board his or her individual boat, and be put to sea equipped with all the necessary provisions—except a compass and map.

The children arrive at the dock. They babble excitedly as instructors direct them to their boats and show them how to operate the motor and other equipment. "Only one to a boat," a chief instructor says. "You may steer your boat as you wish. A group of you may want to travel in a fleet, or you can motor alone if you wish. Just follow your feelings."

Some of the children's parents have warned them to watch out for dangerous reefs, treacherous straits, and islands populated by cannibals. "That's good," the chief instructor says, "but remember you're independent of your parents and on your own now. You make the decisions. The sea has changed since your parents made their voyage. You select the direction that seems best for you."

So the children are launched in their frail little boats while their parents stay home with mixed feelings. Most parents—remembering the wise guidance they had when setting out on their voyage of life—trust the schools implicitly.

But some have heard disquieting reports: the schools have changed; children are being poorly equipped for this voyage. Students are being sent on their own without maps or a compass. But these troubled parents cannot afford to moor their children in safer ports. So they must, by law, send their children to this marina and trust that all will be well.

The children are launched. The instructors fly overhead in helicopters, gauging their progress. Look, there's little Johnny, headed toward an underwater reef. His boat will smash! He could be drowned! But don't worry, an instructor sees him and surely will wave him back. Wait!

Has the instructor gone mad? He is telling Johnny, "Keep going in the direction you feel is right!"

There is Jane, the dimpled little apple of her daddy's

eye. Jane is traveling with a group toward an island of cannibals. Surely her instructor will warn her and her friends. No, he simply circles overhead, shouting, "Go with what the group thinks is right."

Absurd? Ridiculous? Improbable? It happens every day! This parable parallels exactly what is occurring in our humanistic schools. Young children are being taught there are no moral absolutes, no fixed rules of life; they're being dispatched into the world to find their own way. This fact confronts us in every report we hear on juvenile behavior. Rising sexual promiscuity, vandalism, drug abuse, thefts, assaults, drunken driving, and suicides all point to problems in the schools.[2]

What causes some public educators to feel so detached from guiding their students morally? Precisely their philosophy of education! What we believe affects everything we do. Note the following statement in one textbook:

Modern physics teaches us that there are no rules that apply everywhere under all circumstances. Nothing seems certain anymore. If the universe cannot be fully comprehensible to us, how much less certain must we be about our theories of human nature, government, history, and morality? If scientists must be cautious in formulating theories about nature, how much more cautious and tentative must we be in framing conclusions about humans and their society?[3]

Against such a floating life philosophy, the Christian school offers a powerful spiritual advantage, namely, the multiplied opportunity for "teachable moments" to emerge. They surface with regularity because the Christian school provides a context in which biblical discussion of issues is not only permissible but strongly urged. Such a school multiplies the probability for spiritual decision making during the prime years of childhood.

Education for Life

During his first term, President Reagan announced on one of his radio addresses that the Justice Department would file court briefs to help expand the rights of school officials to enforce discipline. The National Institute of Education, he said, reported in 1978 that three million secondary school children had been victims of crimes in schools each month. The study also reported that each month 6,000 teachers were robbed, 125,000 were threatened, and 1,000 required medical care.

Parents who send their children to Christian schools are often accused of "sheltering" those children from the real world. Do we accept the President's description of public education as the real world? Is that the kind of environment in which Christian soldiers are trained and godly minds stirred?

To the contrary, the idea of "sheltering" works just in reverse. Dr. Roy Lowrie, long the Headmaster of Delaware County Christian School in Pennsylvania and now a faculty member at Grace Theological Seminary, argues the case quite differently.

> Sheltering occurs when public school students are not taught that man is made by God. God made Adam out of the dust of the ground, then He made Eve out of Adam. And, every baby from Cain until today is just as much the creation of God as Adam and Eve. It is sheltering to teach that man is an animal.
>
> Public school students are sheltered when they are taught that man is basically good. The real world shows that man is basically evil; something is inherently wrong and is not changed by education or environment. The front page of today's newspaper

will depict the human heart and reveal its depravity. Students do not see this real problem when there is no teaching about sin.

To be sure, some public schools, particularly in rural areas and small towns, still permit godly teachers to share their Christian lives and values with students on a regular basis. May their tribe increase and may God bless their every effort. Let not people in those towns think, though, that such schools are by any wild imagination the standards for the nation! Our kids are in trouble—big trouble. According to Sharon Sheppard,

> During the next 30 minutes, 40 young people will attempt suicide, 57 kids will run away from home, 14 teen-agers will have abortions, 685 teens (all regular drug users) will take some form of narcotics. According to *Time* magazine, nearly one of every five 15-year-old girls has had sexual intercourse. An Associated Press report stated that an "epidemic of crime and disorder" has resulted in 282,000 students being physically attacked and 112,000 robbed each month in America's public schools.[4]

Thank God there is an alternative—biblically and spiritually oriented education in a Christian school.

Chapter 13, Notes
1. Beverly LaHaye, *Concerned Women for America Newsletter*, July 1986, 2.
2. Mel and Norma Gabler, *What Are They Teaching Our Children?* (Wheaton, Ill.: Scripture Press, 1985), 98-99.
3. Marvin Perry, ed., *Unfinished Journey: A World History* (Boston: Houghton Mifflin Company, 1983), 461.
4. Sharon Sheppard, "What's a Parent to Do?" *The Standard* (76:8), 7.

CHAPTER 14

Are There Educational Advantages to Christian Schools?

AMERICAN taxpayers are currently paying $278.8 billion annually for the day-to-day operation of the nation's public schools, more than all other nations of the world combined. The yearly cost of educating each public school student ($4,263) is more than triple that of educating a Christian school student, whose tuition averages $1,300.

Yet in an academic competency test comparing American public school sixth graders with their counterparts in seven other Western industrialized countries, we fared poorly. "American public school students ranked last in mathematics and not much better in science and geography. One-fifth of the sixth-grade students tested could not even locate the United States on a world map."[1] In April, 1983, the National Commission on Excellence in Education issued its historic report, *A Nation At Risk*. The Commission warned that "the educational foundations of our society are presently being eroded by a rising tide of mediocrity that threatens our very future as a nation and as a people."[2]

No wonder the American people seem to sense the need for a new direction in their schools. In one survey of public opinion, 83 percent favored the "back to basics" movement in education."[3] Pollsters asked parents who send their children to public schools, "Suppose you could send your eldest child to a private school, tuition free; which would you prefer—a private school or a public school?" Of the respondents, 45 percent preferred private schools, 47 percent chose public schools, and 8 percent were undecided. That nearly half of public school parents prefer the nation's private schools must be disturbing to the public school community. Those who chose private schools cited as reasons "higher standard of education, better discipline and more individual attention."[4]

Basic Learning Skills

Christian families are opting out of public schools not only because of their anti-Bible, anti-Christian bias, but also because of their weak emphasis on basic learning.

The following report comes from the "Educator's Newsletter," produced by Northern Illinois Gas Company:

> A rising number of middle-class families are reluctantly deserting public schools because they are unhappy with the quality of the education.
>
> Many parents, putting a higher premium on fundamentals, want the more challenging curriculum offered by many private schools. They also like the small classes, heavy homework loads and the easy access to teachers.
>
> Since 1970, as the total number of U. S. school-age children declined, enrollment in non-sectarian private schools had advanced 60 percent to 1.8 million.

Shocking as it may seem, the National Assessment of Educational Progress found that only 42 percent of seventeen-year-olds tested could figure the area of a square when given the length of one side. A Ford Foundation study says federal programs aimed at wiping out illiteracy have failed. As many as 64 million Americans may lack the reading and writing abilities needed for today's technologies.

Paul Cooperman's book, *The Literacy Hoax,* exposes the academic decline of secular education. Cooperman writes:

> I have recently met high school graduates in San Francisco who did not know where the Pacific Ocean was, or whether New York was east or west of California, or how to spell the name of our country. Each year I meet dozens of parents who are shocked to discover that their children read three, four, or five years below their level. With skills down, assignments down, standards down, and grades up, the American educational system perpetrates a hoax on its students and on their parents.[5]

New York senator Daniel Patrick Moynihan reports that 14 million American children live in poverty and more than one-half of American children live with one parent. The school dropout rate, he claims, is 25 percent overall and 50 percent for blacks and hispanics. Moynihan believes that we may be the first generation in the history of America in which the children are worse off than the parents.[6]

Functional Illiteracy

At a time when adult functional illiteracy runs epidemic in America, Christian school educators are committed to the student's ability to read, write, compute, and grasp common concepts. Education has always been essential for believers to follow such biblical directives as, "Look in the scroll of the LORD and read" (Isaiah 34:16) and "Do your best to present yourself to God as one approved" (2 Timothy 2:15).[7]

Many Americans seem to be unaware of the magnitude of the problem of illiteracy in the United States. In a recent edition of *Education Week,* Rudolph Flesch wrote that the U. S. Senate was seeking to set up a national commission to study illiteracy, which is at an appalling level.[8] This is the state of American education in general after a century of compulsory school attendance.[9]

Fortunately such dismal news is not the case with Christian school education in America. According to Dr. Raymond White, Director of Educational Services for ACSI, standardized achievement test scores indicate that Christian school students are performing approximately one year and four months ahead of the national norm. The test (Stanford Achievement Test) is administered each year to more than 130,000 students attending ACSI member schools.

The higher scores of Christian school students may be explained in part by a certain selectivity among Christian school students and a higher degree of parental interest in their schoolwork. While these are factors in the higher scores, the full story includes the academic impact of Christian school teachers who love God, who love children, and who have an unswerving dedication to quality education for the next generation.

A Reasonable Balance

Academics, however, should not be emphasized to an extreme. Christian education should focus on the entire person. Sometimes parents, teachers, states, and even nations get caught up in "academic excellence," and they pressure students beyond their capabilities. The issue is balance. As a nation we need to raise the quality of education in our schools. Most Christian schools have not yet reached their full academic potential. Students need a reasonable amount of pressure to move from comfortable academic zones to new heights of intellectual challenge. The key word is *reasonable*. Most youngsters will respond to a reasonable level of pressure from parents and teachers who lovingly inspire and persuade them that learning is essential to living in our complex world.

The Christian school is able to be more focused, less diffused in its academic programs. It is not under the constant pressure of society to be all things to all people as is the public school. Frequently the Christian school has smaller classes, a higher purpose for learning, greater advantages for small group activities, and a much greater chance for the student to participate in extracurricular events such as athletics, music, and drama. The quality of faculty dedication and the lower faculty/student ratio enable the Christian school to commit more time to its primary tasks.

Perhaps the issue here centers on priorities. Yes, the Christian school takes pride in its academic levels, but that is not the reason for its existence. The central focus is the application of the Word of God to every aspect of study. To be sure, the contrast is dramatic. According to *Insight* magazine, high school dropouts, once a dilemma, are now a crisis.

> Some 27 percent of the United States' teen-agers, or 3/4 of a million, fail to graduate from high school, the NEA says. The dropout rate in large cities exceeds 40 percent, and in New York City it is more than 50 percent. More than half of prison inmates are dropouts.

Kids drop out of Christian schools, too, but at a much lower rate. Committed parents, praying teachers, a majority of Christian peers, considerably strong discipline, and numerous other factors combine to offer the Christian school as a superior academic alternative. Superior buildings? No. Superior equipment? No. Superior in the recognition that education for Christians centers in the mandate of 2 Corinthians 10:5: "and we take captive every thought to make it obedient to Christ."

Chapter 14, Notes
1. Congressional Testimony, "Child Abuse in the Classroom," 400.
2. National Commission on Excellence in Education, *A Nation At Risk*, 368-69.
3. Gallup Polls of Attitudes toward Education, 1969-1984, a topical summary, 32.
4. Ibid., 31.
5. Paul Cooperman, *The Literacy Hoax* (New York: William Morrow and Company, 1978), 18.
6. Daniel Patrick Moynihan, *The Chronicle of Higher Education*, 10 December 1986, 27.
7. Literacy is vital to the Christian way of life. Illiterate Christians are at the mercy of others who interpret Scripture for them. Literacy also helps protect the church against heresy. The decline in basic literacy in the United States represents a major threat to America's Christian community. The overall achievement level of Christian school students offers a commendable deterrent to that decline.
8. Rudolph Flesch, *Education Week*, 12 June 1985, 28.
9. Providing basic literacy to the next generation is not an insurmountable task. Barbara Bateman of the University of Oregon writes: "Near failure-proof methods for teaching all children to read are . . . available. Continued failure of schools to employ these programs is at best negligent and at worst malicious."

CHAPTER 15

How Will Our Child Benefit Socially from a Christian School?

M OST Christian schools offer a positive, safe, caring environment for children. Commitment to holistic education extends beyond classrooms, hallways, and gymnasia to the day-by-day realities of life. Christian schools provide significant social advantages for students in addition to their spiritual and academic benefits. Let's explore six.

Quality Friendships

A Christian school provides students with an opportunity for a much wider range of Christian friends than they would find in public or home schools. In 1970, national Sunday school enrollment was 40,508,568; in 1986 it had dropped to 26,589,251—a decline of 34 percent.[1] Is it possible that this loss occurs largely because most young people attend public schools, and the influence of their non-Christian friends draws them away from the church? I have seen no specific research, but the conclusion seems logical. Meanwhile, the Christian school strongly supports the church and the home.

Friends are the single most important factor in shaping the lives of students in the middle and upper levels of education, and the percentage of Christians is higher among students in Christian schools. Of course, Christian school young people sometimes do link up with bad company among their campus peers, but the potential for such negative peer pressure is much less.

But what about the argument for toughness in spiritual warfare? Shouldn't Christian children learn to "slug it out" in an alien, secular environment? Dr. Clyde M. Narramore, one of the nation's leading Christian psychologists, once said, "A tree planted in poor soil doesn't have the advantages of one planted in good earth. Contrary to some beliefs, we do not grow through resistance. Children do not develop because they resist food. Their growth comes as a result of good food and care."[2]

Wholesome Social Activities

Students attending a Christian school may confidently enter into its social activities because the school's social program will normally be pleasing to God, to the Christian home, and to the evangelical community. Similar social activities in the public school often run counter to Christian standards.

Certainly it is necessary to say here that every parent needs to exercise careful discretion in the selection of even a Christian school. Social standards differ; and since parental authority is the ultimate concern, examine each potential school until you feel comfortable that its standards are compatible with your own.

Minimal Racial Discrimination

Even though a higher percentage of minorities attend public schools, those who attend Christian schools generally experience less racial discrimination. That may be surprising to some who have read or heard that the rapid rise of evangelical schools has been caused by the establishment of "white-flight academies." True, the unrest created by desegregation and busing programs caused parents to search for alternatives; but studies show that Christian schools have come into existence primarily for spiritual and academic reasons.

In his study of Christian schools, Peter Skerry, a Harvard University graduate student, concluded, "these schools were established primarily out of religious, not racial, convictions (parents were concerned about 'creeping humanism' and moral relativism in the public schools) and the quality of instruction they offer matches or exceeds that given in most public schools."[3]

In 1981, James Coleman, a contract researcher for the National Center for Education Statistics, reported that a higher percentage of minority students attend public schools, but that minorities who attend private and religious schools "are substantially less segregated in the private sector than in the public sector."[4] In other words, segregation is a greater problem in public schools than in private and religious schools.

The "Coleman Report," a federally funded research project, revealed the following:

1) Private schools provide better character and personality development than public schools.

2) Private schools provide a safer, more disciplined and more ordered environment than public schools.

3) Private schools are more successful in creating an interest in learning than public schools.

4) Private schools encourage interest in higher education and lead more of their students to attend college than public schools with comparable students.

5) Private schools are more efficient than public schools, accomplishing their educational task at lower cost.

6) Private schools have smaller class sizes, and thus allow teachers and students to have greater contact.[5]

A Safer Environment

I have already noted numerous statistics about the problem of violence in public schools. There are incidents of violence in Christian schools as well, but the contrast is remarkable. Public school students are regularly confronted with threats of violence, and uniformed guards are often needed in the hallways. But Christ makes a difference not only in the academic environment and the spiritual environment of the Christian school, but also in its social environment.

A Minimal Exposure to Drugs, Alcohol, and Tobacco

If students are intent on finding drugs, alcohol, and tobacco, they will do so in any environment. Once again, however, probability favors the parents of children attending Christian schools. Offenders are generally expelled or suspended, depending on the circumstances. Students are taught to resist sinful habits through exposure to God's Word:

> But now I am writing you that you must not associate with anyone who calls himself a brother but is sexually immoral or greedy, an idolater or a slanderer, a drunkard or a swindler. With such a man do not even eat (1 Corinthians 5:11).

Also,

> Do you not know that your body is a temple of the Holy Spirit, who is in you, whom you have received from God? You are not your own (1 Corinthians 6:19).

Rejection of "Values Clarification"

Values clarification in secular education centers on inviting impressionable children and young people to make a choice among options without any consideration of absolute truth and absolute values. Is lying acceptable? Is stealing permissible? Should premarital sex be approved? Well, "it depends." Situations differ. If young people have "clarified" their own value systems and have chosen to do or not to do these things, education has been achieved.

Many public school students are exposed to such secular ideas in sex education classes. In Christian schools, values are already clarified in the inerrant and authoritative Word of God. Rather than being pressured into forming self-made standards of conduct with no moral foundations, Christian school students are urged to surrender their wills to God's unchanging truth and values.

The contemporary values-clarification movement is a bit like giving teenagers a driver's license without a handbook or training, placing them in a car and telling them, "Anything you do on the freeway is okay, just as long as you understand why you're doing it. The important thing is that you have made the decisions." The destructive result of such a philosophy would create automotive lunacy on the highways. On the moral highway of life, values clarification is educational lunacy.

Perhaps the number one problem in public education is the attempt to educate students without a moral point of reference. With a floating target of truth and the desertion of absolutes, the entire system has abandoned its base.

Christians accept the Bible as the only valid moral point of reference for living. It applies to every area of our lives, including the social dimension. Christian school students, therefore, have the advantage of a "driver's handbook." To be sure, possession of an infallible Bible is not possession of an infallible interpretation of that Bible, and Christian school educators must never confuse the two. Nor does the existence of an infinite God guarantee an infinite knowledge of that God. Social standards, however, must have a base in truth, morality, ethics, and values. The Christian school attempts to build its programs, flawed though they may be at times, on that eternal foundation stone.

Chapter 15, Notes
1. Win Arn Growth Report, no. 19, 1987, p. 1.
2. Quoted by Paul A. Kienel, *Reasons for Christian Schools*, Association of Christian Schools International, 1981, 113.
3. Peter Skerry, *Christian Schools, Racial Quotas, and the IRS* (Washington, D. C.: Ethics and Public Policy Center, 1980), 1.
4. James Coleman, *Public and Private Schools*, (Washington, D.C.: National Center for Education Statistics, 1981), 43.
5. Ibid., 2.

CHAPTER 16

How Will Our Family Benefit from Enrolling Our Child in a Christian School?

IT is not necessary for children and young people to be immersed in the world of sin and evil in order to be inoculated against it. My own two children have attended Christian schools almost all of their lives. Not only have they received a superior education and developed wholesome friendships, but now as adults, they have no apparent desire to conform to the world. They remain as enthusiastic as their parents about their years in Christian school.

As a professor of Christian education for almost thirty years, I have traveled thousands of miles in behalf of Christian schools. I have visited scores of Christian school classrooms and talked with hundreds of Christian school educators and parents. The Christian educators' enthusiasm for their work and their Christian commitment is an undeniable fact. Why subject children to a negative, unreal world when a wellspring of positive Christian school education, one that that is at harmony with parental concerns, is available in what a growing number of Americans refer to as "God's School System"?

Paul B. Smith, pastor of People's Church of Toronto, the largest Protestant Church in Canada, once said,

> If I had my life as a pastor to live over again, I would warn my people constantly about the dangers of the North American public school system. Over a period of 30 years I have watched with a heavy heart the devastating effects of the public schools, both on my own children and those of many of my congregation.[1]

A School-Family Partnership

Many Christians have lost faith in American schools because the public school community has become insensitive to the Christian family and to biblical values. It is not the absence of anything that makes a public school an unacceptable environment for a Christian child. It is rather the presence of what Gordon Clark once called "a systematic, day-by-day inculcation of secular humanism as a philosophy of life." The philosophy of public education stands contrary to the Christian view, and secular humanism affords a genuine threat to Christian families.

Remember that Christian educators don't oppose public education per se. For the secular individual in a secular society, the American system of education may be the finest that has ever existed in the history of the world. But Christian children are not secular individuals. They are citizens of a different country with a different set of values, a different set of standards, and a different idea of truth. When we parents give our sons and daughters to the state for education, we invite the values, standards, and untruths of a godless cosmos to penetrate their spirits, and that is not healthy for any family, especially the Christian family.

Occasionally, public school leaders launch frontal attacks on the family and those who hold to traditional values. For example, Paul Kienel reports the following statement by a Harvard professor, offered as a part of his speech at a seminar for teachers:

> Every child in America entering school at the age of five is mentally ill, because he comes to school with certain allegiances toward our founding fathers, toward our elected officials, toward his parents, toward a belief in a supernatural Being, toward the sovereignty of this nation as a separate entity.
>
> It's up to you teachers to make all of these sick children well by creating the international children of the future.[2]

Christian schools support the traditional values espoused by most Christian families. Public education often creates an adversarial relationship between the family and the school. Such conflict ought not to occur in a Christian school.

Curriculum Control

Parents, more than ever, should be concerned about the academic level of instruction in the schools their children attend and about the textbooks to which they are exposed. Many Christian schools teach from textbooks written by Christian authors—for academic reasons and to escape negative prejudice. Many secular textbooks reflect a strong bias against the family, the church, and in some cases, against our government.

The secular textbook publishers are currently reeling from an independent study of ninety of the most commonly used secular textbooks for grades 1 through 12 in the public schools. The study was conducted by Paul C. Vitz, a professor at New York University in New York City, and funded by the U. S. Department of Education. Dr. Vitz describes his project as follows:

> The purpose of this project was to systematically investigate how religious and traditional values are

represented in today's public school textbooks. The general finding is that public school textbooks present a very biased representation of both religion and of many traditional values.

I used the methodology of "content analysis" to examine a representative sample of widely used public school textbooks. All results were verified by outside, independent evaluators.[3]

Dr. Vitz documents that religion, a vital part of American history, has been almost eliminated from our children's textbooks. Moreover, the family is undercut or portrayed in ways that are uncomplimentary.

Regarding texts written for grades 1 through 4, he found that "the specific function of these social studies texts is to introduce the students to contemporary American society." Yet there was not one word or image that referred to any form of contemporary Protestantism. Vitz goes on to say, "None of the books had one text reference to a primary religious activity occurring in representative contemporary American life."

What omissions can call forth such criticisms? What significant religious aspects of American history were missing in these books? Vitz lists the great awakenings of the 1700s and of the 1800s; the urban revivals of the 1870s and 1880s; the Holiness-Pentecostal Movement; and the Born-Again Movement of the 1960s and 70s. Evangelical Protestant schools were completely overlooked, and Catholic schools were not mentioned.

In general, none of the textbooks adequately presented the major religious events of the last two hundred years. For example, not one book gave any information that would allude to the historical origins of today's "religious right." Not one text had a word about the turn-of-the-century religious activity of William Jennings Bryan; there was not one reference to such prominent Protestant preachers as Billy Sunday, Dwight L. Moody, or Billy Graham. Even more important was the omission in all these texts of the essential role religion has played in American history.

Christians believe that marriage is the origin and foundation of the family, but such a view was never presented in any of these books. In particular, the words *marriage, wedding, husband, wife, homemaker,* and *housewife* did not occur once. Not one of the many descriptions or comments on the family suggested that being a mother or homemaker was a worthy, dignified, and important role for a woman.

The books did not mention a single instance of people giving time or money to charity (for example, no family budget included funds for charity), much less for church contributions.

The ninety textbooks Dr. Vitz and his research team studied are used by more than 60 percent of the nation's school children. A high percentage of what a child learns in school comes through textbooks. The result? Approximately thirty million youngsters will know almost nothing about the role of religion in American history. In addition, they will have a distorted view of the American family. The prevailing bias in many public school textbooks is clearly anti-family, anti-church, and anti-traditional values.

Family Values

Traditional family values are important in contemporary education, and the contact between parents and the school must be strong, with mutual respect expressed. Despite frequent arguments to the contrary, it is the public school student who is sheltered from reality. In the foreword to one book about Christian schools, newscaster Paul Harvey wrote,

> Years ago it was argued that students maturing in a "sheltered environment" would, like hothouse plants, be unprepared for the cold outside world.

Now, more and more Americans are realizing that it is, in fact, the public or state-school student who is "overprotected." He is "sheltered" from religious instruction and exposed to all forms of non-Christian philosophy and behavior.[4]

Christian parents would rarely if ever send their children to a non-Christian Sunday school or to a Unitarian church to fulfill their God-given responsibility to bring their children up "in the training and instruction of the Lord" (Ephesians 6:4). Yet 80 percent of the evangelical community, ignoring all the warning signs, plunge on with their curious loyalty to a public school system which seems to be "the American way."

It is time for Christians to wake up, to shake off their apparent lethargy, and start supporting educational programs which center in God's truth and support, rather than stifle, family loyalty. To be sure, too many parents send their children to Christian schools for the wrong reasons. Unless we have genuinely considered the basic philosophical arguments involved in education, we are not really sure why the money should be spent.

We are merely touching upon family advantages of Christian schooling in the pages of this chapter. Added to everything already said are such important issues as opportunity for direct participation and influence in the school's programs; a relative openness of communication between parents and teachers; the greater likelihood for the accommodation of school schedules to family and church activities; the possibility of brothers and sisters attending the same school on the same campus (of particular importance when both parents work outside the home); and the emphasis of the school on a biblical view of family life and order.

Do we really want the kind of mind-control institution described by Alan Peshkin?[5] Viewing the Christian school movement through the eyes of a secular and skeptical Jewish researcher provides some helpful warnings for evangelicals. His chapter, "Truth's Organizational Structure," should challenge every Christian school to reexamine its philosophic premise. Keenly Peshkin searched for a rationale that could explain to the secular educator the enormous growth and popularity of schools such as Bethany over the past decade. He was forced to conclude that the phenomenon is ultimately not understandable except by those who know experientially the "total world" of commitment to Jesus Christ.[6]

My own awakening as an educator came when I noticed that some of the most outstanding Christian philosophers of an earlier generation were also strong Christian school men, scholars whose lives reflected both intellectual brilliance and spiritual fervor—such men as Frank Gaebelein (Stony Brook School), Bob Smith (Bethel College), and Gordon Clark (Butler University)—these and others have thought keenly through the issues of education and have come to the conclusion that Christian schooling is the most valid alternative.

Chapter 16, Notes

1. Quoted by Paul A. Kienel, "America Needs Bible-Centered Families and Schools" (La Habra, Calif.: ACSI, 1979), 121.
2. Taken from an address given at a childhood education seminar in 1973 by a professor of educational psychiatry at Harvard University. (Reaffirmed by Dr. Kienel in a phone conversation, March 1983).
3. Paul C. Vitz, *Educational Choice*, vol. 2, no. 5, May 1986.
4. Paul Harvey in Paul Kienel, *The Christian School: Why It Is Right for Your Child* (Wheaton, Ill.: Victor Books, 1974).
5. Alan Peshkin, *God's Choice: The Total World of a Fundamentalist Christian School* (Chicago: University of Chicago Press, 1986). For a full review by David Edwards, see the July-September 1987 issue of *Bibliotheca Sacra*.
6. Kienel, *The Christian School*, 7.

CHAPTER 17

How Does Christian School Education Help Society?

THE National Center of Education Statistics released a report December 20, 1984, which grabbed headlines in newspapers across the country. These headlines indicated that there had been a surge in private school enrollment in the 1980s, with one in every eight American students attending a school outside the public system. Families were choosing private education because of their dissatisfaction with the public schools. Many parents were turning to Protestant evangelical schools for the moral and religious grounding they wanted their children to have.

Total enrollment in non-public schools is not available, but the Association of Christian Schools International, the largest of the Protestant evangelical educational groups, reports that the number of students in its affiliated schools grew from 186,000 in 1978 to 390,000 in 1984. Nationwide, the number of Christian schools has grown from several hundred in the 1960s to more than 10,000 today, with close to a million students enrolled. The number of students is growing by nearly 80,000 a year. The increase in Christian schools has contributed significantly to the first nationwide increase in private school enrollment in several decades, according to federal officials.

Christian Schools in the United States

Year	Schools
1965	1,000
1980-81	7,500
1984-85	*13,000

*Projected

Source: Bruce S. Cooper of Fordham University and James S. Caterall of UCLA

Many believe the actual number of Christian schools is considerably higher than the 13,000 reported in the *Washington Post* graphic. A publisher of Christian school curriculum materials recently sent a team of workers to the Library of Congress to obtain the name and address of every Christian school listed in the nation's telephone directories. They uncovered 32,000 evangelical Christian schools! Whatever the actual number, the force of Christian school education in our society can no longer be questioned.

A Healthy Alternative

This rather lengthy introduction to this chapter emphasizes a crucial point: Christian schools are good for society because they offer an alternative.

In their book, *The Emerging Order*, Jeremy Rifkin and Ted Howard claim that "the growth of Christian schools is truly one of the most significant cultural phenomena of the decade." In this study of sociological and religious trends, the authors state,

> What makes the Christian school movement so utterly mind-boggling is that it has begun to seriously

undercut a century-long (humanistic) trend in popular education in America. Before the Civil War, most popular education was firmly embedded in an evangelical Christian framework. With the rise of industrial capitalism and the emergence of the modern era, education became increasingly secularized and institutionalized in the public arena. For the past half-century, our public education philosophy has rested on a set of principles that include: professional control over school administration, curriculum and teaching procedures; a secular humanist approach to learning; and the ultimate primacy of scientific truth. The Christian school movement has turned this educational philosophy out, in favor of a Christian-based philosophical approach to education.

In practice, this means that over a million school children in America today are receiving a completely different interpretation of the basis of knowledge, truth and reality than their counterparts in public schools.[1]

Theistic Commitment

Christian schools are also good for society because they reflect a traditional and foundational commitment to God. As I have said repeatedly, the prevailing philosophy of public education centers in secular humanism, which teaches the supremacy of man rather than the supremacy of God. Christian education re-establishes the primacy of the Creator.

In his popular broadcast "Focus on the Family," James Dobson released the results of a survey he conducted among a thousand of his listeners. Survey results indicated that Christian parents give the public school system only a 48 percent approval rating compared with a 71 percent approval rating by the general public, as determined in a 1980 Gallup poll.

By contrast, the survey showed that 88 percent of Christian parents approve of their children's Christian schools, with only 6 percent registering disapproval. Dr. Dobson told his listeners, "Although this survey would not meet the rigors of the scientific method, it would appear that Christian parents are far less satisfied with public education than their non-Christian counterparts, largely because of humanistic trends in recent years." In commenting about the future of public education, Dobson warned,

> If Christian parents are to be enticed to keep their children in the public system, then educators must become more sensitive to the values of the Judeo-Christian ethic. Public schools can't be expected to teach Christian doctrine—nor should they—but they can create an atmosphere in which basic Christian beliefs are not contradicted. Educators' failure to do so will result, in my opinion, in the death of public education in America.

In an effort to regain parental confidence, public schools (with the help of generous taxpayers) may make a modest academic comeback. Comeback or not, though, most will continue to be secular, spiritually sterile institutions. The dominance of secular humanism can be easily established from its own sources.

> I am convinced that the battle for humankind's future must be waged and won in the public school classroom by teachers who correctly perceive their role as the proselytizers of a new faith: a religion of humanity that recognizes and respects what theologians call divinity in every human being. These teachers must embody the same selfless dedication as the most rabid fundamentalist preachers, for they will be ministers of another sort, utilizing a classroom instead of a pulpit to convey humanist values in whatever subject they teach, regardless of the educational level—preschool day care center or large state university. The classroom must and will

> become an arena of conflict between the old and
> the new—the rotting corpse of Christianity, to-
> gether with all its adjacent evils and misery, and the
> new faith of humanism. . . . It will undoubtedly be
> a long, arduous, painful struggle replete with much
> sorrow and many tears, but humanism will emerge
> triumphant. It must if the family of humankind is
> to survive.[2]

Obviously, not all public school educators subscribe
to such a viewpoint, but many do. Certainly the preceding
paragraph would have a far greater chance for acceptance in the public schools than in those offering a Bible-
centered education which acknowledges the lordship of
Jesus Christ.

Leadership Training

Christian schools are good for society because they
are producing Christian leaders for tomorrow. In a stir-
ring article entitled "The Fourth 'R'," Paul Parsons, a
professor of journalism at Kent State University, reports
on his analysis of one hundred Christian schools in sixty
cities. The article is no whitewash, and many of the problems of Christian schools are pinpointed.

Nevertheless, one of the common denominators
Parsons found in the schools studied was the stress on
discipline and traditional values such as respect for authority, honesty, punctuality, and character qualities. He
notes that "the vast majority of students in Christian
schools are there by choice." "When it comes to the
spiritual atmosphere and the values taught amid
academic lessons, the schools and students are in agreement." The article ends with a quote from one of the
Christian school educators interviewed by the author: "If
we can make Christian schools strong enough academically but not too narrow, they may very well produce the
leaven to reproduce Christian values in our society."[3]

Emotional Stability

Christian schools are also good for society because they can provide a deterrent to childhood depression, which often leads to suicide, a growing national problem. By the power of the Holy Spirit, godly teachers can offer students hope and a purpose for living (Psalm 78:7).

Children are people. They have many of the same fears and concerns as adults but lack the maturity to handle them. Sometimes young people get depressed to the point of irrational behavior as extreme as suicide. Most adults realize periods of depression will end and they endure them, but children often see no end to depression and attempt acts of desperation. In *Christian Home and School,* Stefan Ulstein addressed this national scandal in an article entitled "Teen Suicide: Beyond the Mask."

> Suicide is the second largest killer of American teen-agers, surpassed only by accidents. Over 5,000 teen-agers killed themselves in America last year, and it is predicted that each day in 1985 another 18 will follow them. Add to this the more than 50,000 who attempt suicide each year and the scope of the epidemic becomes sadly clear. In 1960 the rate of teen-age suicide was 5.2 per 100,000; by 1980 it had soared to 12.3 per 100,000 and it may still be climbing.[4]

My impression is that Ulstein's statistics are carefully conservative, as the American Academy of Pediatrics reports that the adolescent suicide rate has tripled in the last twenty-five years.

The best protection against childhood depression is to let each child know he is a unique creation of God and that God loves him and offers caring protection. Often the most influential adults in the lives of children, outside the family, are teachers and principals. Godly educators provide stability to secure the emotional well-being of students.

Another way Christian schools offer emotional stability is by being a deterrent to childhood loneliness. The U. S. Department of Labor estimates that "there are 32 million children of all ages (infant through high school) who have mothers working outside the home. Thirteen million of those children are under age 14. Each year, an additional four percent of the nation's mothers take outside jobs."

In the August 15, 1986, issue of *The New York Times Magazine,* Louise Bernikow reported that current studies reveal "the physical and emotional consequences of loneliness pose greater dangers than anyone thought. And loneliness may have a larger impact on society than we have realized. Adolescents appear to be more plagued by loneliness than anyone else."[5]

Lonely children are often distressed with the thought that no one cares and no one loves them. Christian school educators have the opportunity to express personal love and concern for these lonely students in their classes; they can also share the truth that Jesus really does love them and "is a friend who sticks closer than a brother" (Proverbs 18:24).

Congregational Support

Christian schools are good for society because they can be an integral part of the local church. Obviously, education always benefits the broader community, thereby strengthening both child and family. The church benefits as well. A higher level of biblically trained children and young people can enhance the quality of any local congregation. To be sure, there are definitive problems in dealing with Sunday school students, some of whom attend Christian schools and some of whom do not. When a church sponsors and houses a school, equipment use can be a constant headache for the administration of both phases of the program. These are not unsolvable problems; they present challenges to making the Christian school more effective in its support of both church and society.

Public schools may profess pluralism as a goal, but that pluralism tends to focus only in ethnic, social, or methodological domains. True philosophical pluralism in public education is being methodically stamped out. As Hodge once said, "He who believes most always yields to him who believes less; and he who believes less will eventually yield to him who believes nothing."

Coming to Faith

Finally, and of greatest importance, Christian schools are good for society because Christian school educators can and do lead students to trust Jesus Christ. The Bible, prayers, witnessing, songs, displays on bulletin boards, Bible studies— all believed by most to be illegal in public schools—develop an awareness of the Savior in Christian classrooms. The result is that many students come to faith. Following a formula established in a national survey, ACSI estimates 250,000 students accepted Jesus Christ as Savior in America's Christian schools during 1986. The potential for social good in that kind of evangelism is overwhelming.

The social value of Christian education ultimately finds its way into the lifestyle of students. David Roth argues for not only the integration of faith and learning, but the integration of faith, learning, and living.

There is the idea of going beyond faith and learning to applying it. FAITH. One's faith must be understandable, clear and sincere. There must be a biblical perspective for one's faith in the Lord Jesus. It cannot be encumbered or watered down by man's rules and additional input. LEARNING. Learning is important. God expects us to use our talents. We're to rise to the potential that is innately ours. It is unbiblical for a Christian to despise or avoid learning because of slothfulness or other distractions. LIVING. It is possible to have solid faith, be well-educated and not be able or willing to apply it in everyday life. Living is the capsheaf—the culmination of a life of faith and learning. Living one's faith, applying one's education is the bottom line.[6]

Chapter 17, Notes
1. Jeremy Rifkin and Ted Howard, *The Emerging Order: God in an Age of Scarcity* (New York: Ballantine, 1983), 128.
2. John Dunphy, "The New Faith of Humanism and Teachers," *The Humanist Magazine*, January-February 1983, 26.
3. Paul Parsons, "The Fourth 'R'," *Christianity Today*, 4 September 1987, 21-27.
4. Stefan Ulstein, "Teen Suicide: Beyond the Mask," *Christian Home and School*, March 1985.
5. Louise Bernikow, "Alone, Yearning for Companionship in America," *The New York Times Magazine*, 15 August 1986, 24.
6. David Roth, *ACSI International Newsletter*, August 1987, 3.

CHAPTER 18

What Do I Need to Know about the Financing of Christian Schools?

HAVE you seen the bumper sticker that reads, "A mind is a terrible thing to waste—support your public schools"? Apparently it is meant to imply that the worth of a child is centered in his mind. Education is important because that child might someday become a great scientist, a brilliant musician, or an important national leader. A child's mind becomes something of a national and natural resource, a wise investment for tax dollars, because it will someday be of value not only to him but to the overall wealth and power of the nation.

Of course a child's mind is important, but the Bible teaches that it cannot be separated from his eternal, living spirit. I make no distinction here between the term "soul" and "spirit," as they seem to be interchangeable, particularly in the New Testament (John 12:27; 13:21, NASB). The fact which Christians must recognize, however, is that the immaterial part of man is accounted for only in Scripture. Evolutionists have no satisfactory explanation even for the mind of man, much less for his soul and spirit.

The Value of a Child

Christian education views people holistically with what can best be described as an image-of-God perspective. The evangelical view of sin in no way minimizes its deep respect for the genuine dignity of the creature made in God's image. Dr. Robert Lightner reminds us that:

> The believer is a representative of God on earth. Therefore, it becomes his duty and solemn responsibility to those who have not been renewed in the image of God through Christ to share the gospel of God's saving grace. Man lost something in the fall, but not the image of God. His personality was marred, but not destroyed. Fallen man in the image of God is so marred and depraved because of sin that only God's grace can restore.[1]

Some will ask, "But what does all this have to do with school financing?" Let us begin by understanding the inherent value of every child. Even a little one abandoned by one or both of his earthly parents is still loved by his heavenly Father. Obviously, it is incumbent upon all Christian parents to provide their children with the best possible training—education that can be honestly characterized as "training and instruction of the Lord" (Ephesians 6:4).

Some Christian parents will choose not to send their children to Christian schools for philosophical reasons; and if they have thought through all the issues and honestly come to that conclusion before the Lord, they are doing the right thing. Others will be unable to send their children to Christian schools, either because there is no Christian school near their home or because the costs are prohibitive. A much larger category of parents, however, has either not thought through the issues or stands unwilling to pay the added expense.

The Availability of Christian Education

Christian school education could and should be available to all families. Many cannot afford it. But the schools themselves cannot shoulder the full blame for that unfortunate reality. In most cases, they practice economic responsibility, provide scholarships where possible, and solicit charitable giving from donors in the community. In an article in *Christianity Today*, Paul Parsons describes Living Word Christian School in Manhattan, Kansas. "The school also doesn't have tuition. It requires a tax-deductible 'donation' to the church of roughly $80 a month per child. According to Principal Gary Ward, 'This isn't a private school operated as a business on the side, it's a ministry of the church.'"[2]

It is safe to say that the Christian community in general does not do enough to help its own poor. Our response to the needs of the poor is hardly commensurate with the spirit and action of the New Testament church (Acts 4:32-35). Giving does not mean just food relief programs and clothing for destitute families. The church could do a great deal more to assist its children in obtaining quality Christian education.

Options for Financing Education

Many families could simply rearrange their financial priorities to pay for their children's education at a Christian school. Contrary to the common argument that Christian schools are havens for the rich, Christian schools represent an economic cross section of American society because of the modest tuition they charge. According to the Council for American Private Education, "As a group, the parents of private school children belie the image of an affluent elite. Sixty percent earn less than $20,000 a year."

Some think Christian schools do not charge enough. Some families could comfortably pay more than they are paying, and the balance could be gathered into student scholarship funds for families who are genuinely needy.

Still another option being exercised by more and more schools is joint relationship with a local church. The great advantage here is sharing facilities. Such a situation can be awkward, but it has financial advantages.

What role can small businesses play in financing Christian education? The big foundations are committed to the big institutions, and private universities, particularly prestigious ones, virtually exist on that kind of money. Perhaps the Christian man who owns a little body shop over on Main Street might be approached for some regular funding for Christian education. If we look hard enough, there may be some viable alternatives to asking constantly from the same group of people— parents.

As I draw this section of the book to a close, let me emphasize the realities of choice. The enemy of the Christian school is not the federal government, the state board of education, the public school system, and certainly not the home school. In recent years, some educators who have complained the most about humanism have tried the hardest to take various fields of government into their own hands. In short, they attempt to defeat humanism by acting like humanists!

The real enemies of the Christian school are the substandard Christian schools which flaunt their mediocrity in the name of Christ; teachers and administrators who attempt to carry out their spiritual duties by fleshly ability (2 Corinthians 3, 4); our own lack of commitment and our comfortable affluence which prevents us from making the kind of sacrificial commitment necessary to realize Christian schooling in its fullest possible extent; and the blatant barbarism of contemporary culture.

In my opinion, as the Christian school strengthens its commitment to excellence and demonstrates its concern for biblical priorities, it will increase its credibility not only among the evangelical community, but throughout the country. We are like Paul in Athens. Rather than scorning or vilifying pagan philosophy, he offered the Athenians something better—the life-changing, spirit-enriching, family-strengthening message of biblical Christianity. Almost twenty years ago, the governor of California addressed a gathering of Christian school educators in that state. Ronald Reagan said,

> It is essential to our further educational system that private schools thrive. The private institution often serves as a pacesetter, an educational whetstone helping to hone the educational process and forcing the public system to compete in a drive for excellence. Your institutions are very much needed. You are a part of the bulwark of morality that is so essential to the foundations of freedom. God is not dead on your campus.

Chapter 18, Notes
1. Robert P. Lightner, *Evangelical Theology* (Grand Rapids, Mich.: Baker Book House, 1986), 173.
2. Paul Parsons, "The Fourth 'R'," *Christianity Today*, 4 September 1987, 24.

CHAPTER 19

David Smith's Response to Kenneth Gangel

READERS of the Christian school section will quickly become aware of Kenneth Gangel's commitment to his beliefs. He shares with us that he has served for thirty years as a professor of Christian education. He is thoroughly convinced that God wants your children to enroll in a Christian school.

To bolster his convictions, Dr. Gangel quotes extensively from Scripture. A careful reading of each of these verses is a reminder of our responsibilities as parents, as Christians, and generally, as citizens. These verses, however, offer little specific support for the Christian school movement.

Buzz words are seemingly added to elicit a negative emotional response from readers. The author uses anti-public school phrases such as, "anti-faith environment," "secular paganism," "servanthood versus pleasure-seeking and self-centered," "humanistic and pagan," "secular missionaries," "state-controlled schools," "victims of mayhem," "menace to society" and "anything goes." These and other comments in their context are meant only to discredit those associated with public education.

Unfortunately, the author's sources for public school information are individuals who are highly critical of and have little direct contact with local schools. He quotes extensively from Christians who speak and write as outsiders with regard to public school realities. How much better it would have been for the author to have actually spoken with evangelicals who are serving as teachers, administrators, and board members and in other roles in our schools! Instead of talking to these Christians, he largely dismisses them and includes them among those who "stray from the words of knowledge" (Proverbs 19:27).

Dr. Gangel, using information from Paul Kienel, takes the liberty to condemn public education based upon an alarming quotation from an eccentric Harvard University professor. This teacher who has little knowledge about, or experience with, public schools is quoted as saying that "children possessing traditional values are sick and need to be fixed." Then, he uses quotes from *Humanistic Magazine*—"proselytizers of a new faith" and "rotting corpse of Christianity"—to associate public schools with evil.

Using such statements from a non-public school university professor and quoting a leftist magazine to condemn public schools does not help to provide a proper assessment of public education. It is unfair when Christian school writers condemn all of public education by quoting from a few isolated non-representative extremists.

The author liberally makes comments that are open to question and debate. Dr. Gangel, for example, accuses Horace Mann of using public education to weaken America and to introduce non-biblical instruction. Most historians would disagree. We read that those attending public schools are becoming adjusted and conformed to the world in violation of Romans 12:2. We are also told that Christian schools are America's best formula for evangelism. Only Christian schools expose students to the real world, and Christian schools are the best hope for transforming society.

The author states that the Christian school movement is growing at the rate of three new schools a day. He implies that America is in the middle of a mass exodus from public education. While a growth in the number of these schools is occurring, the total enrollments are quite small. Many of these so-called new schools will enroll as few as twenty to thirty children spread across six or even twelve grades.

Approximately 10 to 12 percent of our children are in private education, with only about 1 percent actually enrolled in fundamentalist Christian academy schools. The last time America witnessed a growth of these small church schools was in the late 1950s and 1960s. These church schools were usually for whites only and were established to retain a segregated subculture.

The author believes that teachers in Christian schools love children and try to understand the uniqueness of each child. I am sure this is true. Unfortunately and inaccurately, Dr. Gangel leaves the impression that public school teachers are somehow different and less caring.

I have the privilege of interviewing teachers who want to join our faculty. Not only do we hire Christian teachers, but I have also interviewed several Christian school teachers who would like to join with the public schools. I believe that, for the most part, all teachers generally care about the uniqueness of each child.

The statement is made that Christian schools are good for society because their students are seldom involved with anti-social behavior. This is true, of course, but it is a little bit like a rooster taking credit for a sunrise.

Christian schools tend to enroll students whose parents are caring and concerned individuals who value education. Students enrolled in public schools who have loving parents who value education will also be unlikely participants in anti-social behavior.

It is true, as Dr. Gangel states, that students in private and Catholic high schools are more likely than public school students to graduate, enroll in college, and persist in post-secondary studies once enrolled. Again, this may well be more the influence of the family than the school attended.

Dr. Gangel blames the public schools for a host of problems. Is there any church or family problem that is not conveniently placed at the local schoolhouse door? Rather than looking for scapegoats for church problems, it would be better for churches to ask about the quality of prayer, fellowship, unity, commitment, and the strength of Christian family life within each congregation.

We read that Christian schools operate with far less money than public schools. This is true, but I do not believe this should be viewed as necessarily a positive trait. Public schools spend more money per child primarily because they provide more opportunities for all students, including the mentally gifted, mentally retarded, and the physically disabled. This costs money, as does the comprehensive curriculum offered to regular students. Athletic opportunities and courses like calculus, college-level history, electronics, computer programming, and welding are examples of what is usually unavailable in Christian schools. Finally, many churches can keep Christian schools' costs low by muzzling the oxen. Many of these small schools save money by not paying their teachers even a modest income.

Last year, there were two new Christian academy schools within my central Indiana community. One enrolled forty students and the other nine. Using the Accelerated Christian Education curriculum, both claimed to provide a good education from first through twelfth grades. These Christian academies, while virtually identical, were unable to negotiate the formation of a single school. Influence within the community, church resources, and the education and social adjustment of children were sacrificed when the public schools were abandoned.

Forty-five hundred Christian schools nationwide use the Accelerated Christian Education Program. The ACE curriculum is now a $15 million a year operation used by a quarter of a million Christian school students. It is probably the most widely used curriculum in Christian schools. The ACE authors claim, "we prepare a child for life from God's point of view."

This ACE philosophy is representative of a large portion of private Christian academy curricula, embraced uncritically by many church school officials. ACE undermines curiosity and encourages a blind adherence to a very narrow world view. Rarely progressing beyond a low memory level, the aim is not to encourage students to think for themselves but rather to tell them what to think.

Dr. Gangel fails to warn his readers that Christian schools, like public or private schools, vary substantially in quality. I believe there are good Christian schools that are making significant educational and spiritual contributions to the lives of Christian young people. I also believe there are Christian schools of poor quality.

If parents decide to follow Dr. Gangel's advice by leaving their neighborhood public schools, I would encourage them to examine carefully the needs of their children in connection with the services offered by the church schools under consideration. In a search for a Christian school, the following questions may be helpful.

1. How, and to what degree, does the school combine Christianity with other subject matter?

2. What are the teachers like? What is their academic training? How were they selected and how long will they

stay with the school? Are they committed both to students and to Scripture?

3. What are the school rules, and how are they enforced?

4. Does the school have a philosophy and/or doctrinal statement of purpose? Ask to see it.

5. Ask to see and review a copy of a written curriculum. A curriculum guide should include current information on what a student is expected to learn in each subject area.

6. What kinds of children are enrolled? Parents differ on what they expect of a student body background. Look for students from different social classes and backgrounds. Are certain minorities excluded? Do all of the children come from Christian homes? You may want to request the names and actually talk to parents with children enrolled.

7. What are the national standardized tests used by the school, and how successful are students on these exams?

8. What special programs exist for either gifted children or children with learning problems? If you have average children you may want to ask how instruction is individualized to meet the specific needs of each average child.

9. What textbooks and other materials does the school use? Do the teachers use current editions of the materials?

10. What role do you have in working with the school for the common goal of educating your child? Are parents expected to be partners with the school in areas such as discipline and spiritual and academic development?

11. When may you visit the campus while school is actually in session? Plan to speak with students, teachers, administrators and other employees, such as maintenance staff.

Referring to the three educational options presented in this book, Dr. Gangel says, "the real question is which is most biblical." His answer for all parents is that the Christian school is the only proper and, indeed, the only biblical answer. I, of course, disagree. Individual parents must evaluate prayerfully what is best for their children in many aspects of life, including schooling.

Our responsibility is to participate in and to influence our public institutions. However, we must respect parents who, for whatever reason, have found it necessary to remove their children, at least temporarily, from public school. I respect the commitment that Kenneth Gangel and others have made to serve the needs of these people.

Some will find it necessary because of local circumstances to leave the public school. Some will begin home schools while others will remain in public school. The question is not which of the three school systems is biblical but, rather, which learning environment is best for your child and your family. Whether we send our children to public, Christian, private, or home school, I hope we will respect and support each other as Christians and Americans.

CHAPTER 20

Gregg Harris's Response to Kenneth Gangel

Dr. Kenneth Gangel is an excellent scholar and educator who has encouraged thousands of Christian school parents, school administrators, and teachers in his career. He is also a respected student of God's Word who believes that "All thoughts of man expressed in written or spoken word, his ideas, his sciences and his philosophies ought to be scrutinized by the measure of their accuracy in the bright light of God's Word." To this I heartily agree—as well as with his arguments in support of a distinctively Christian education.

Dr. Gangel's overview of the history of education is as accurate and concise as I have seen. I believe it verifies my position that public schools and compulsory school attendance laws from the period of the Roman emperor Julian on have been used as a weapon of religious warfare to change the religious world views of children. Our disagreement over the place of schools in Israel and the early church is important, but it does not set aside the substantial agreement we have on other points.

According to Dr. Gangel, the purpose of the Christian school is to expose students to the real world as seen through the eyes of God and to instill in those students solid defenses against a conformity to the unreal world of the secular community. I realize that in context Dr. Gangel is referring to the contrast between the ungodly indoctrination of the public school system and the bibliocentric instruction of a Christian school. However, I must take up the issue of the "real world" referred to in this statement.

As I will show in my discussion of home schooling, the primary principle of education in God's Word is companionship. Those who walk with wise men will be wise, but the companion of fools will suffer harm. The design of the Christian school, with its use of age-segregation, is an artificial world, not the real world as created by God.

I agree with the arguments Dr. Gangel has presented in support of Christian education. However, the inefficiency of the public schools' approach to instruction—specifically the classroom and the use of peer groups—has been borrowed by the Christian schools. This is far removed from the principle of children walking with wise men. It encourages children to become closest companions with their young and inexperienced age-mates in the Christian school. Christian students may be capable of making good decisions, but there is still the need for chaperoning their interaction. As Dr. Gangel knows very well, not every Christian school student is a model Christian.

He says that children are gifts of God to parents and that parents, not the state or federal governments or even the church, are responsible for the education and training of their children. Children do not belong to their parents, they belong to the Lord, but they are entrusted to their parents as a sacred stewardship. The Christian schools could act on this conviction in a much more direct way. They could support parents in their educational responsibilities instead of encouraging them to abdicate that responsibility by placing their children in a school.

Dr. Gangel states that the government and the church can and should be supportive of parents in their responsibility to carry out their mission as primary educators of their children. But the statement that schools as they are now designed exist to provide that support sounds like the argument that restaurants exist to support the culinary skills and responsibility of the home. Let's be honest. Schools have to pay the bills. Economies of scale enter in. A certain size student body is needed to support a conventional school.

Education in modern civilization has become a product to be bought and sold, just like shoes and clothing; parents are no longer expected to take the time to produce these items on their own. However, human education, like human medicine, must never be treated like just any other product. The stakes are too high.

Certain basic principles must be honored in relation to human beings, no matter how expensive it may be to do so. In medical practice, human life is sacred. That is an absolute. But what is the corresponding absolute principle in human education? Children need to be companions of their wise elders, preferably their parents. Just as the devaluation of human life in medicine has had dire consequences in society (abortion, euthanasia, and infanticide) so age-segregation is having dire consequences among our youth (drug abuse, sexual chaos, racial alienation, and psychopathy).

If children are intended by God to be with their parents, and parents are intended to be wise, then by taking children out of the home we reduce the motivation for parents to be wise. We also deny children the opportunity to walk with what could have been the wisest people in their lives, canceling their hope of having a sure sense of heritage. Schools by their structure do the opposite of what they intend. They encourage parental neglect.

Dr. Gangel states that the Christian school allows parents to bring their children up in the nurture and admonition of their Lord, not in the nurture and admonition of man as taught in the secular schools. He says that what the children are taught should be a direct extension of the parental view, that parental values should guide the hiring of teachers. He states that the teachers should be those whom the parents would hire themselves, and the lifestyle of the teachers should be a direct extension of the lifestyle parents would lead before their children. He believes that the spiritual and social standards of a child's teacher should be in harmony with those of the child's parents. I agree. And this can be best accomplished when parents are encouraged and equipped, by the schools and the churches, to be the teachers of their own children. The Christian school's talk does not line up with its walk.

A Friendly Proposal

My suggestion to Dr. Gangel and others in the Christian school community is that they embrace a new design, one that will truly fulfill the purpose he has stated so well. Why not blend the home school and Christian school movements into one innovative educational hybrid?

For instance, I suggest that every Christian school make its teacher training programs open to parents. Teach parents how to teach all the major subjects of study. Teach them the methods as well as the philosophy of instruction. Let your schools become community colleges for the entire body of Christ to draw upon. Why limit your services to children?

I suggest that the Christian school library be equipped to give parents access to the best materials for use in home instruction. If the schools would like to operate educational supply stores on site, I would be delighted. Carry all the major lines of curriculum. And sell these at a reasonable profit to those who want them.

I suggest that the Christian school host various home school events, such as curriculum fairs, standardized testing of all students on school grounds, home schooling conferences, and interschool student competition in sports, the arts, and the sciences. Debating teams could use a few home school students. If you would only include us in what you normally do for your classroom students, that would be enough. We have done well on our own, but we recognize the value of what you have to offer. And we are willing to pay a fair price to have access to these things.

The Association of Christian Schools International has already led out in this way by including a few home school exhibitors and speakers in their Christian school conferences throughout the country. ACSI has for the most part maintained a close and friendly contact with home school leaders these last four or five years, and because of this, the rapport between the home school and the Christian school community is growing stronger all the time.

Finally, I suggest that the local Christian school teacher be encouraged to serve as a consultant to the home school families in the community. If properly oriented to this facet of Christian school ministry, teachers could provide a tremendous encouragement to many families—helping them with their instruction and discipline needs, assisting parents in finding the best teaching materials, and as a third party, assuring objectivity in decisions. This could be a second income for such teachers, or an extension of their current job description as a school teacher.

Simply put, if the Christian school leaders honestly believe God has called them to assist parents in their role as the primary instructors of their students, then it is time for them to put their resources to work to help accomplish that goal. Redesign your school system from the top down. Begin to encourage home instruction in those families where it is possible. Equip the saints for the work of this ministry. Your conventional classrooms will continue to be needed. Parents whose lifestyles and careers require an out-of-home program will need the conventional approach. With a much smaller student body on campus and a large network of home school extension families scattered throughout your community, you could have greater impact at less expense. One such school in Orlando, Florida, Circle Christian School, is administered out of a church office with no campus at all. This is a model any church could follow.

I am willing to do all in my power to help schools and churches move in this direction. I realize it will take time. I have consulted with the executive board and staff of the largest Christian school association in the world, ACSI, and they have responded with great warmth and cooperation. From the very beginning, all pastors and Christian school administrators have been offered a free pass to the Home Schooling Workshop, anywhere in the U.S. or Canada. Hundreds have attended. But thousands have not. The offer is still open.

In the home schooling movement, we don't expect everyone to jump into everything suddenly. We are patient planners. We find that "after-schooling" and "summer-schooling" offer very popular thresholds to a full-scale home-school lifestyle. We are willing to be just as patient with the Christian schools. The Christian schools could perhaps operate evening and summer programs to assist families. The relationship will grow from there.

The opportunities for support and cooperation between these two is unending. It is simply a matter of providing leadership and developing the vision necessary to work out the transitions. Interpersonal conflicts are sure to erupt whenever different points of view are brought into contact with one another. This book is an example that mutual respect and understanding are possible. Conflicts can be resolved in time. Ultimately, the home school and the Christian school can become integral branches of a complete system of Christian education that derives its strength from the godly home.

PART 3

HOME
SCHOOL EDUCATION

Gregg Harris

CHAPTER 21

Is There a Biblical Basis for Home Schooling?

IN the long run, the most important thing we may ever do in our lives is raise our children.

No matter how dedicated we are to serving God in our lifetime, our children will probably be our greatest contribution to God's purposes. For one thing, they will probably outlive us. And, what's more, as adults they will either continue to build on the foundation we have started, or like Solomon's son Rehoboam (1 Kings 12:1-17), they will unwittingly tear apart everything we have spent our lives trying to build. Our short-term gains, however great, can be wiped away by the next generation. And we won't even be there to stop them.

This means that our ultimate vote for what the future holds is found, not in how we cast our ballot in the next election, but in the character of each child we release into this world. Psalm 127:4 tells us our children are like arrows—strategic weapons to be aimed for life, at targets pleasing to God. We've got to make every shot count.

But how do we train up our children in the way they should go? What aims a child for life? Can we wield that degree of influence over our child's future? And would we be violating his individuality by doing so?

Aiming our children for life is God's idea (Proverbs 22:6). We hold legitimate sway over our child's direction in life, and if we hesitate to use our influence, God's enemies will certainly have no qualms about using theirs. They will steal our arrows and aim them at targets of their own choosing. If God has issued our children to us, we are the ones who must aim them.

The Purpose of Children

To understand the biblical basis for anything related to children, we must first identify the biblical reasons for having children. Unfortunately, much disagreement has crept into the church over this question. There is little consensus left. Scripture is all too often interpreted in light of clearly unbiblical presuppositions from thoroughly secular authorities.

Not that this is new. The church in every age tends to become a product of its current cultural context, hence the need for repeated reformation and revival. But if worldliness means being conformed to the world's systems of thought instead of to the spirit of Christ, then the church in modern America is remarkably worldly. George Barna and William McKay of the American Service Bureau write, "Survey data supply ample evidence of the bankruptcy of the commonly held world views of Christians. It is undeniable that as a body American Christians have fallen prey to materialism, hedonism, secular humanism, and even to a jaded form of Christianity that rejects much of the commitment required of faithful servants."[1] This worldliness in the evangelical church's thinking colors its understanding of children and the education of children. Even the Christian school community must strive against creeping secularism within its own ranks.

But in the Bible the original purpose for children was to help Adam and Eve fulfill God's commission to take dominion of the earth in order to tend it for His glory. Godly children are the primary means by which the godly householder subdues the earth (Genesis 1:26-27). Such dominion does not mean mankind should rape and pillage his environment, but it does involve putting the creation to its intended use. The basic purpose for children then is to multiply the godly and subdue the earth in righteousness. This purpose is given several times in Scripture, and it is always addressed to mankind at the point of replenishing the earth (for example, during the times of Adam and Noah).

The Great Commission of Matthew 28 is the spiritual counterpart to the purpose of children. The church is called to multiply the children of God by evangelism. Discipleship (i.e., the education) of those born into the family of God is an integral part of God's overall design. Children, whether biological or spiritual, need to be prepared for their responsibilities in life. Children are necessary for the fulfillment of God's purposes on the earth. And so Christian education finds its proper place in the ministry of the family and the church.

Families are therefore important in God's eternal plan. In the Bible we find great emphasis placed on family cohesiveness, loyalty, and continuity. Like Abraham, a father honors God when he directs "his children and his household after him to keep the way of the LORD" (Genesis 18:19). Children are inevitably molded by the companionship, example, instruction, and discipline inherent in family life. God calls his people to be righteous and to have children who will continue the pattern after their fathers have gone on to their reward.

Returning to Psalm 127, the godly man who intends to build his household and faithfully guard the interests of his community is directed to consider the impact well-trained children can make. God issues each child to his parents just as a Commander-in-Chief issues arrows to his troops. Arrows must be sharp and they must be carefully aimed.

The concept of "aiming children as arrows" focuses our attention on the balance in biblical child training. Academic considerations are of great importance. The arrow must be sharp. But intellectual sharpness will be of little value if the child is unwilling to pursue his life purpose faithfully. The moral development of the child, and the preservation of his sense of identity as a member of his own family and of God's larger family, is critical. If a child lacks a clear sense of moral direction, his scholarship cannot fulfill its purpose. Because the primary objective of having children is to extend the impact of the godly householder's life on the world, character training is at least as important as academic training.

In a world that is at war with God, Christian education is rearming the church for battle. That is why the non-Christian world takes so dim a view of Christian schools and Christian home schools. Both are strategic maneuvers in God's battle plan. And because this is so, the approach to education used by Christian parents must be fundamentally different. Any approach that is compatible with this world's distorted understanding of the purpose of children will be unacceptable to the Christian parent.

The Goal of Christian Education

The goal of Christian education is a *life*, not a living; it has much more than vocational training in view. Making a living is important, but only because it underwrites the normal expenses of living the life. Secular education encourages us to place making a living on a higher level of priority than living the life God has called us to live. It asks us to serve mammon in place of God. The life God calls us to is one of single-minded love and devotion to him (Deuteronomy 6:4).

While this world is busy reducing education at all levels to "vocational training" and "human resources development," the Bible urges the Christian to respond to the higher calling of God in Christ Jesus. John Milton, the great sixteenth-century Puritan and author of *Paradise Lost*, wrote in his treatise "On Education": "The end then of learning is to repair the ruins of our first parents by regaining to know God aright, and out of that knowledge to love him, to imitate him, to be like him. . . . I call therefore a complete and generous education that which fits a man to perform justly, skillfully, and magnanimously, all the offices, both private and public, of peace and war."[2]

If our goal was merely to process a future labor force, like so many head of livestock, the conventional classroom system might suffice. But because we have a higher view of mankind, the typical school's system of comparing student with student, identifying employment potential, categorizing, labeling, career tracking, and grade manipulating, is totally unacceptable. Because the adventure of the Christian life is fundamentally different from that of the world, we require a fundamentally different approach to education. God has given us a tall order. How does he intend for us to accomplish it?

The Power of Companionship

Developing a fundamentally different approach to education requires us to rethink, biblically, the role of parenting in the overall education of children. First we must identify the basis of our influence in our child's life, and then how we can use our influence intentionally to effect his life's direction. The answer from the Scriptures is as simple as it is profound. The foundational principle of education in the Bible, and the one which I believe holds the key to our success in developing an appropriate system of education for the body of Christ, is *companionship*. This is the force that aims a child for life.

The power of companionship is revealed in such passages as Proverbs 13:20, "He who walks with the wise grows wise, but a companion of fools suffers harm." Paul warns the Corinthians, "Do not be misled: 'Bad company corrupts good character'" (1 Corinthians 15:33). Our Lord makes the observation that "everyone who is fully trained will be like his teacher" (Luke 6:40). The "unschooled" apostles were honored by their enemies with the recognition that "these men had been with Jesus" (Acts 4:13). The awesome power of companionship influences moral discretion and molds every facet of human personality. Without reservation, companionship is the ultimate educational force.

This idea is bound to shake up the educational establishment because it takes us back to square one. But if it's true that companionship will direct the course of a child's life, then providing wise companions for a child is the essential challenge of a Christian education. And when God goes looking for those responsible for the training of children, his list is short: "Parents" (Ephesians 6:1-4).

If, as the saying goes, "Values are better caught than taught," then companionship provides the context for this to take place. Parents are called to be wise companions for their own children. They are also responsible to protect their children from harmful companions. But in such companionship, what is the occasion in which values are "caught"? How do companions make the hand-off? And what exactly is being handed off?

Touching the Palate

Proverbs 22:6 illuminates the occasion for handing off our values. "Train a child in the way he should go, and when he is old he will not turn from it." The word translated "train" in this proverb can include the rendering "touch the palate." It is an idiomatic usage picturing a common household scene. When a small child is weaned from his mother's breast and onto solid food, the Middle Eastern mother has no baby-food grinder. Instead she personally chews the baby's food at each meal. During the meal, she discreetly reaches into her own mouth and draws out a dab of the very food that delights her own palate and this she touches to the palate of her child. On this intimate occasion the baby shares with her the things that she enjoys, and by doing so, meal after meal, he develops tastes for certain foods—tastes that will never go away.

The writer of this proverb has the inner workings of companionship in view. God is showing us the occasion for handing off a value. A taste for our delights, whether good or evil, is imparted to our children as we enjoy them together. And whatever we enjoy, we tend to talk about.

Listen to us describe what we enjoy to our companions. We touch their palates with words that are the overflow of our hearts. Investors talk about their investments. Sports enthusiasts talk about sports. Artists talk about art. No one is surprised by this. Our actions may speak louder than our words, but our words carry tremendous clout, especially when they harmonize with what we do.

Delight

But what exactly is being handed off in this "touching" process? What has the power to influence a child "when he is old?" The word *value* comes to mind; so does *character*. Both are useful terms, but a more accurate answer, according to God's Word, is *delight*. Psalm 111:2 tells us, "Great are the works of the LORD, they are pondered by all who delight in them." People study the things that delight them. Even when we are old, we make time to pursue the things we have developed a taste for. We pursue them independently—for the rest of our lives.

When school was finally out for you, what did you continue to "study?" In other words, what are your delights? For a clue, look at the books and magazines you make time to read. Like everyone else, you are a delight-directed student. It will be the same for your children. They will step into their adulthood to pursue certain tastes and delights. Delights they caught from their companions at home—or somewhere else.

A Christian home is to be filled with wholesome delights. A child's world should best be described as "delightful." Art, music, science, and literature should be his. For the sake of the children, let family reunions, parties, and hobbies of all kinds stake their legitimate claims on our busy schedules. Such activities and festivities can be facilitated in even the humblest of homes. For Christ's sake, we must learn to take time to "smell the roses" with our children. We must be their companions and use the occasion to impart our delights to them.

Our Father deals with us in just this way:

"Delight yourself in the LORD and he will give you the desires of your heart" (Psalm 37:4).

"If you remain in me and my words remain in you, ask whatever you wish, and it will be given you" (John 15:7).

"For it is God who is at work in you, both to will and to work for His good pleasure (Philippians 2:13, NASB).

As we walk with him, he imparts his delights to us, and then he provides us with every opportunity to satisfy our heart's desire. This is "the training and instruction of the Lord" (Ephesians 6:4).

Back to Deuteronomy 6

Companionship instructs a child's heart as nothing else can. It instills life-long delights that comprise the framework for all study. Attitudes, convictions, values, and whatever else comprises personality are influenced by companions and their delights.

The question is, who will touch the palates of the next generation of young Christians? With whom will they converse most intimately, and whose delights will become the topic of their life-long study? If we would raise up devoted Christians, our course should be clear. We must provide devoted Christian companions for our children.

The principle of companionship is more fundamental than even the principle of parental responsibility. Parents can choose to be either good or bad companions to their children. Not all parents are wise. In Deuteronomy 6:6-7 Moses takes this into account when he announces, "These commandments that I give you today are to be upon your hearts. Impress them on your children." God begins by addressing the heart condition of parents. If God's commandments don't happen to be on our hearts at the moment, we are not thereby relieved of duty. Rather, we are given the assignment to put these things on our hearts immediately. As parents we must delight in God's Word and study it in order to become the wise companions our children need.

"Impress them" or "teach them diligently" (NASB) removes all room for lackadaisical, "happenstantial" instruction. The term is impregnated with a sense of purpose. In modern home schooling, clearly defined goals and lesson plans are used to hold ourselves accountable. Firm direction of studies is expected by God.

But since the instruction is going on in the home and between a parent and his or her children, the brusque tone is taken away. Straitlaced rigidity is not needed. Like all things spiritual, home schooling is joyful but intentional obedience to the Word of God. The joy of learning is not smothered by a sense of obligation. The context of the home ensures that the learning will be accomplished on a flexible schedule. It has to be because homes, unlike classrooms, are part of the real world where life comes at you from all directions at once and without much warning.

Immediately following, in Deuteronomy 6:7, we find the classic description of parental companionship: "Talk about [God's commandments] when you sit at home and when you walk along the road, when you lie down and when you get up." What are "these commandments" which Moses gave Hebrew parents to teach to their children? What topics of study did they include? A reading of the Book of Deuteronomy reveals a complete and well-rounded curriculum. While offering more than ten chapters of history, the book also addresses various aspects of art, warfare, marriage, childbearing, economics, ecology, criminal justice, education, health, agriculture, government, poverty, safety, ownership, dress codes, business, self-defense, dietary rules, singing, the attributes of God, and much more. In other words all aspects of a godly life are required subjects of study. The curriculum of "the life" is life itself, life as lived by one who is older and wiser.

The best context for learning about life from a wise person is simply to be with that person. Sitting at home, walking along the road, lying down and rising up are all part of our routine. As parents, we are called first to be wise, and then to include our children in our wise routine. Truly Christian education is an apprenticeship energized by the power of godly companionship. And the best place to enjoy this kind of education is in and around the home.

If the most important thing you may ever do is raise your children, then wisdom suggests that you be the one who raises them. If your children must be influenced by the power of companionship, wisdom demands that it be your companionship which holds the greatest sway in their lives. This companionship is called "Christian home schooling." And provided you are willing to be a wise and devoted parent, it is the best route to take.

Chapter 21, Notes
  1. George Barna and William McKay, *Vital Signs* (Westchester, Ill.: Crossway Books, 1984), 140.
  2. John Milton, *Complete Prose Works* (New Haven: Yale University Press, 1953), 2:377.

CHAPTER 22

How Did
Home Schooling Begin?

TEACHING children at home is not a recent educational fad. The historical roots of home education go all the way back to the original members of society, the first family. Obviously Adam and Eve were the only teachers their children knew. But since then, in most cultures and time periods, the child's tutors were his parents and the home was his primary schoolhouse.[1]

From antiquity the training of children has been viewed as both a religious responsibility and an economic necessity. In many ancient cultures, any child who grew up to be unbelieving or unskilled was shunned or even executed. Failure to train one's children in both areas of life was a serious offense against the whole society. The Jewish Talmud states that if a father doesn't teach his boy a trade, he teaches him to steal.

Old Testament Israel

When God gave his covenant law to Moses, he established parental instruction of children in the home as the norm for Israel (Deuteronomy 6:4-9). That brought literacy to its highest value—to read and understand God's Word. Although ancient Israel had a high literacy rate, they also maintained their oral traditions. The Israelites used their annual feasts and fasts, which commemorated important events from their past, as an opportunity to educate within the home. Holy days were designed specifically to encourage Hebrew children to ask questions of their parents. God designed into the Jewish home by law regular opportunities for meaningful home instruction (Exodus 13:14).

During the captivity in Babylon, when the Jews had no temple at which to worship, they devised the synagogue system to maintain biblical literacy and worship. This alternative was possibly learned from the Babylonians. Whatever its origin, initially this innovation only supplemented ongoing home instruction.

After the Israelites returned to their land, they continued the synagogue schools. In doing so they deviated from the Deuteronomic commandment, separating religious instruction from economic training. This set the stage for the scribes and Pharisees to later become a professional caste of teachers, first of religion, and eventually of basic literacy. A division between the sacred and the secular aspects of life began to appear. Faith and works were slowly divorced, and legalism rushed in to fill the gap in Jewish culture.

Hebrew culture had no compulsory attendance laws for synagogue schools. The voluntary association of ten or more Jewish households established and maintained a synagogue. Therefore, the authority of the synagogue school teacher, or rabbi, over the children came from the parents, not the priests. In many ways the synagogue schools were educational co-ops for the Jewish families. Just as parents attended the services on the Sabbath by choice, they voluntarily sent their children to the synagogue schools on weekdays. Still, the Jews maintained strong convictions about training their children at home.[2] Their use of the synagogue was supplemental to the ongoing character instruction and trade skills provided by each child's father and mother in obedience to the Law of Moses.

Schools in the New Testament Era

In the New Testament era, the education of Christian children continued to be centered in the home. Early Christians were mocked from the very beginning for being simple and for believing what seemed to scholars of the day to be a simpleminded faith. Yet Clement of Alexandria is representative of the church fathers' view that the Christians were doing very well in spite of their lack of credentials and polish: "Almost all of us, without training in arts and sciences and the Hellenic philosophy, and some even without learning at all . . . have through faith received the word concerning God, and been trained by self-operating wisdom."[3]

The early Christians were generally a humble and unlettered people. What their heathen opponents meant as mockery, the Christian apologists turned into a boast (1 Corinthians 1:26-29).

First-century churches were home churches. Early Christians understood that the church was not intended to be a school for children but a place of worship and instruction for Christian adults. This was in keeping with the original design of the church to equip the believers for the work of the ministry (Ephesians 4:12). Thus the early church was a support system for godly households and individuals.

For the next three hundred years the home remained the primary place of study and instruction for children and the church itself continued to be a "home church." As a result, even under recurring persecution, the Christian household and the church continued to be strong and faithful.

The Schools Become a Battleground

After the first four centuries, the history of education became intertwined with the history of church and state competition. Emperor Constantine's conversion in A.D. 312 made Christianity legal. With the state's acceptance of Jesus Christ, Christianity was taken captive as a new civil religion. Ultimately, the church would become the new state, and the Roman clergy would become a powerful extension of the government.

Soon, the early Roman Catholic church began to wander from the authority of Scripture, replacing sound biblical doctrine with its own rapidly growing system of tradition. As the Roman church gained greater political power, Roman Catholic education became a political tool. Knowledge is power, and depriving the common man of basic literacy and even a knowledge of history became a means of securing the corrupted church's power. Education became a means of hiding the truth from people.

The Protestant Reformation

It should not be any wonder that one of the first things the early Protestant reformers ignited was a renewed interest in the literacy and education of the masses. The ability to read, and the availability of the Bible in the reader's native tongue, became the surest path to the renewal of true Christianity. But just as the Jews borrowed too freely from their captors in Babylon, Christian education was profoundly affected by its captivity under the church of Rome.

The Protestant Reformation introduced a radical new use for schools; compulsory indoctrination. German leaders were ready for an occasion to pull away from the Holy Roman Empire. Religious reformation would put an honorable face on what otherwise could be viewed as a political revolution. It would also knit the threads of society together for resistance of whatever reaction came from Rome. Luther was indeed a godly man, but he was also practical. In 1524 he asked for the establishment of public schools and compulsory school attendance. Eventually public schools were established in every town.

In Luther's day compulsory attendance laws were intended to turn Roman Catholic children into Lutheran children, against the will of their Catholic parents. In our day similar laws are used to turn every child, regardless of religious faith, into atheists. Compulsory school attendance laws are effective weapons of religious and ideological warfare.

Fortunately, other aspects of child training were not taken away from the home. Skilled trades continued to be passed down by fathers in the home or through guild apprenticeships. The favored classes also continued to assume the task of educating their own children in academic as well as economic skills. The nobility employed servant tutors to teach their children, and occasionally they permitted a bright peasant child to join them.

Schools in America

In America, freedom of religion was eventually established by federal law. The new nation began its adventure in liberty without the aid of government schools. With the exception of a few common schools in New England, education in the United States took place in homes or in private schools. Parents trained their children at their discretion, choosing the method of instruction and the curriculum with the same liberty they enjoyed when they made any other decision affecting their personal lives.

Yet literacy was very high. John Adams noted in 1765 that "a native in America, especially of New England, who cannot read and write is as rare a phenomenon as a Comet."[4] Not only did families teach their own children in their own homes, they also offered instruction to the village orphans or the children of the exceptionally poor. Out of these "kitchen schools" came some of the greatest leaders and scholars the world has ever known.[5]

In the years that saw great waves of immigration from Eastern Europe and Ireland, many Protestants feared that Catholicism might eventually dominate the political system of America. Early compulsory education laws were enforced primarily in urban industrial centers where the population of Catholic immigrants was concentrated.[6] Rural America was not required to forsake its home school patterns until a later date. According to conventional wisdom, the sons and daughters of the farm and village communities formed the foundation of our national strength. The swelling urban population, with its poor "street urchins" and its organized youth gangs, needed government intervention. The child of the immigrant, with his foreign culture, needed to be melted into Protestant American culture. The child of poverty, enslaved in the mines and the factories, whose parents could not or would not provide education for him, was the real target of compulsory school attendance. The fact that he also had that "popish religion" added impetus to the drive to push school legislation through. Protestant, middle-class America empowered their new public school systems to deal with the immigrant's child, but not with their own children.

This brief social-historical background explains why the public school establishment has so few misgivings about undermining a child's confidence in his family's religious faith. Since public schools were designed from the beginning to change the religion of the student (from Catholic to Protestant), it is not surprising to find public schools currently employed in the same activity. The only difference is that now the public school seeks to undermine all forms of theistic religion in order to convert children to the predominant nontheistic faith of the current school establishment: secular humanism.

Neither should it surprise us to find that public school officials expand their public school powers simply by identifying new social ills to be addressed by their tax supported schools. Utopian dreamers of every liberal stripe find sympathy and funding in American halls of academia. Today you will find nuclear freeze education, New Age relaxation, creative visualization training, sexually neutral role-modeling, child-abuse detection, values clarification, AIDS and "safe sex" education, and birth control clinics in public schools across the U.S.

In the midst of this bureaucratic maneuvering, there has always been a small but faithful band of Christian teachers and administrators. These Christian educators are fulfilling an important ministry to the students who must attend the public schools. I salute them, and I encourage Christian parents to pray for them and respond to their requests for community support. My complaint is not against the teachers. It is against the system, the structure, and the legal basis of the public schools.

The State of the Home Schooling Movement

In the last two decades, Christian home schooling has made important strides. Unlike the Christian schools, home schooling has broken away from the public school's inefficient structure and developed an approach to education that honors the biblical principles of education. So also have families in the secular home schooling community. But the Christian segment of the home schooling movement, which comprises over 85 percent of the total, has also replaced the public schools' anti-Christian curricula with distinctively Christian materials. It is the combination of liberation from the classroom and the public school curricula that makes the Christian home school option superior to all other options in education.

The Christian home school movement is a positive response to the argument that the Bible has absolute authority over all of life. An appropriate education for a Christian must be thoroughly integrated with the Bible and every subject must be studied in the light of God's word.

Home schooling is in a strong position today. Every state has its own local history of home schooling, its own local pioneers and leaders. Curriculum fairs are hosted in every metropolitan area, and home schooling associations, services, and publications are on the increase.[7] My own ministry, The Home Schooling Workshop,[8] is hosted in over thirty cities each year and now has over thirty thousand alumni. Home schooling is a topic in demand, and it is spreading to countries around the world.

The state of the movement is good, but the higher up the mountain we climb, the stronger the winds of opposition blow. There will yet be a major legal battle over who is ultimately responsible for the training of children. And if we lose our right to home school as we believe we should, the Christian school will be next to feel the pressure of government intrusion.

But because of the faithfulness of so many, home schooling continues to be a refreshing attempt to restore education to its proper place in the home. Thousands of years of false assumptions are being stripped away to reveal the simple model given by God in Deuteronomy 6. The Christian expression of what is now the home schooling movement is good fruit. It is born of refreshingly biblical thought on the subject of education. For that reason I believe it will continue to be a valuable force in preparing our children for our Lord's return.

Chapter 22, Notes

1. D. F. Payne, *The New Bible Dictionary* (Grand Rapids, Mich.: Wm. B. Eerdmans Publishing Co., 1970), 336.

2. Michael Steven Shepherd, "The Home Schooling Movement: An Emerging Conflict In American Education" (doctoral dissertation, East Texas State University, 1986), 7.

3. Clement of Alexandria, *Stromateis* 1.20.99.

4. *Diary and Autobiography of John Adams*, ed. L. Butterfield (Cambridge, Mass.: Harvard University Press, 1961).

5. According to John Whitehead and Wendell Bird, constitutional attorneys of our day, nine American presidents were taught primarily through home education. These include George Washington, James Madison, John Quincy Adams, Abraham Lincoln, Franklin D. Roosevelt and Woodrow Wilson.

Home schooling has its Who's Who in every area of accomplishment. Generals Douglas MacArthur and George Patton were home taught in the early years. Writers Phyllis Wheatley, Samuel Clemens, Pearl S. Buck and Agatha Christie were also home schooled. Industrialist and philanthropist Andrew Carnegie studied at home. Intellectual giants such as Benjamin Franklin and John Stuart Mill were trained primarily at home. Inventor Thomas Edison, believed by many modern reading specialists to have been dyslexic, was kicked out of the public school for being "addled" and therefore unteachable. Young Edison devoted himself to his studies at home, instructed by his patient and loving mother.

But these kinds of Hall of Fame lists can be misused. Supreme Court Justice Sandra Day O'Connor is often listed as a home school alumna when, in fact, she only studied at home for seven months, and that only during the first year of school. In our search for members of the Home School Hall of Fame, we must be objective, honest, and less desperate for big names. Those who are drafted into the Home School Hall of Fame should be able to stand up to any amount of scrutiny.

6. Henry J. Perkinson, *The Imperfect Panacea: American Faith in Education, 1868 to 1976*, 2d ed. (New York: Random House, 1977), 69-70.

7. Christian Home Education Associations in nearly every state keep their state legislators constantly on their toes, and vice versa. Most states now have at least one association of Christian Home Educators, though names differ from state to state. For more information about the association(s) in your state you may contact Christian Life Workshops, 180 S.E. Kane Road, Gresham, OR 97080.

The Home School Legal Defense Association is a legal insurance program for all home schooling families. Membership requires an annual fee. For more information you may write to Home School Legal Defense Association, P.O. Box 2091, Washington D.C. 20013.

The Teaching Home magazine is an excellent bimonthly Christian publication for home schooling families. For subscription information write to The Teaching Home, P.O. Box 20219, Portland, OR 97220-0219. Dr. Brian Ray compiles all the most pertinent research related to home schooling in his *Home School Researcher*. Subscription information is available by writing to Brian Ray, c/o Christian Life Workshops, 182 S.E. Kane Road, Gresham OR 97080. Dr. Ray serves as a researcher for CLW and all of the studies referred to in chapters 21 through 28 have been provided by him. Home schooling books, including my own recent offering, *The Christian Home School* (Wolgemuth & Hyatt, 1987) are appearing on the bestseller lists among Christian publishers.

8. This weekend workshop offers a complete orientation to the motivation, the lifestyles, and the resources of a Christian home school. For an up-to-date National Itinerary of the workshop, live and on video, write to Christian Life Workshops, 180 S.E. Kane Road, Gresham, OR 97080.

CHAPTER 23

What Are the Spiritual Advantages of a Home School Education?

OURS is a fast-paced society. Time is precious. And handing down our heritage in Christ to our children is not something to be rushed. Home schooling permits Christian parents to enjoy more time with their children. More than any other option in education, home schooling increases our opportunity to be a family in Christ.

The home schooling household is more effective as the seedbed and the greenhouse of childhood faith. It is a protected place of warmth and nurture. Harsh winds and cruel elements will come later. Even the seedling of a mighty oak needs a season of gentleness to get started.

In the tender years, the home can provide that gentle season. Parents can nurture each child's confidence in God before his confidence is put to the test. At the appropriate time, the home can provide a controlled setting in which to practice hospitality. Through carefully planned get-togethers children can be introduced to people outside their own family without undue risk of harm. The whole world can come for dinner . . . but just a few at a time.

What is the alternative to this approach? Conventional schools expose children prematurely to the conflicting winds of pluralism in American society. Our country is not a melting pot. It's more like a tossed salad, and there are plenty of "fruits and nuts" in the mix. Before the young student's own beliefs are clearly defined and established, he is required to deal with the beliefs of others. Emotional attachments to his new friends begin to create conflicts in his mind.

Because the child's exposure to the world is premature, he begins to wonder whether Mom and Dad really know what they're talking about. No one seems to agree in his classroom. His teacher has as much as said that "No one can say what is right or wrong for someone else." And she acts as if such concerns are not important anyway.

"Ah, but it's different in a Christian school." Is it? There are many different levels of devotion to Christ, and it can be more devastating for a child to meet a nominal Christian, one who does many things the child's parents have told him are wrong, than to meet and interact with an avowed atheist. Haphazard input from too many points of view too early can discourage the child from trying to live out the implications of his faith. Give the child time to put down his spiritual roots. The fruit will be much sweeter in its proper season.

A Heritage of Liberty to Preserve

The liberty to train a child in the way he should go is one of the primary expressions of true religious freedom. Religious freedom includes the right to protect our children from harm. These are the very freedoms that brought the pilgrim fathers to the shores of the New World. Whenever we tolerate the dilution of these freedoms, we abandon the precious liberty our forebears lived and died to secure for us.

Home schooling ends the perennial argument over what should or should not be taught in any particular school: It puts all instruction, including religious instruction, back into the home where it belongs. By using the many new resources and Christian curricula, the home-school family can study every subject, from art to zoology, in the light of God's Word. Home schooling erases the artificial division between the sacred and the secular aspects of life. Faith and works are reunited. All of life becomes a project of delightful study, and all studies are woven together into the tapestry of an all-inclusive Christian world view. What Christian school advocates only envision, the home school delivers. And it delivers this education while pulling the family back together.

Restores Family Unity

Many Christian families find their daily lives fractured. Each member is being pulled in a different direction. Work, church activities, school, and a parade of extracurricular activities for each student place demands on each member's time without consideration for the family as a whole. The hectic pace takes its toll. Parents pass their children and one another like traffic on the freeway. The homes of many have become an empty shell, a place to go when nothing else is open. The Christian family's children are being lost in the shuffle of modern society with its emphasis on individual, often age-segregated, pursuits. James Dobson pointedly asked, "Where's Dad?" Many children today must ask, "Where's everybody?" Who stays home anymore?

In a later chapter I will address the many advantages of home schooling to the family, but the spiritual advantages to the family must be addressed here. Home schooling restores the home as the center of life and faith, for the child and for his parents. It restores a sense of purpose. In an age when the extended family has broken down and the nuclear family is crumbling rapidly, each household must strive to preserve its own integrity. Home schooling not only permits this, it supports it. And along with preservation comes the restoration of several other adventures of family life. The TV is turned off, and in many instances, tossed out. In its place, conversation, hospitality, and community involvement experience a homecoming. Because a biblical education must prepare the child for *all* of life, every aspect of a godly home becomes a necessary educational activity. Families that might not otherwise get involved in the civil, social, or ministry activities, often do so once they begin to home school.

Hospitality and Evangelism

Ideally, the Christian household is an embassy of the kingdom of God on earth. It is maintained and equipped in order to be shared with others. And this can be accomplished without endangering the host's children. Christian families can meet their obligations to their children and to the outside world at the same time through biblical hospitality. And each is enriched by the other.

The Christian home is designed to be a place where neighbors, friends, and even international travelers can taste and see that the Lord is indeed good. Through this balanced approach to hospitality children can be introduced to the wider world of interesting people and still be protected from harm. Many home school families now offer a guest room for this very purpose. They are ready to serve others from a position of family strength.

Home school children have many school presentations to give. For these they need courteous guest audiences. Audiences dominated by children can be dangerous to a child's budding interest in public speaking. Ridicule and mockery are poisonous. Because children are not usually mature enough to encourage a fledgling speaker, it is wise to pack the house with adults who will be more supportive. The right response on the part of the guest audience can "touch the palate" of the home school child with the sweet rewards of presentation and speech skills. This adds yet another opportunity to invite non-Christian neighbors into the home.

But where do we find an adequate supply of guest audiences? Our neighborhoods. Most are full of people who cannot resist an invitation to have dessert and hear a science or history presentation from a home-school child. It is not unusual for our guests to ask us what we believe and why we are teaching our children at home. The door is now open to share the gospel with our neighbors.

Serving in the Church as a Family

The home school's emphasis on doing things together as a family has spawned a growing interest in serving together in church work. Rather than allowing its members to be recruited individually to labor in separate spheres of church ministry, the home school family is likely to request an opportunity to serve together like the household of Stephanas (1 Corinthians 16:15). Not every task can be pursued in this way, but many can. And this approach permits the family to strengthen the relationship between parents and children, while doing the work of the Lord. Children who serve the church in this way are much more likely to develop a healthy perspective on ministry.

In effect, this is an apprenticeship system. Younger, less experienced members of the family develop the skills and knowledge of those who are older and more experienced. The advantages for the church under this arrangement are numerous. Instead of being placed in age-graded youth programs, which tend to teach children to passively consume ministry, the children are with their parents learning how to produce the ministry of the church for others. Children can learn to be effective teacher's aids in the Sunday school program, or assistant gardeners, janitors, and cooks. Whatever mom and dad are asked to do for the church should include their children, as much as possible.

As mentioned earlier, the main purpose of the church is to equip the saints for the work of the ministry (Ephesians 4:12). That ministry is to be lived out in the context of daily life in and around the godly home. By dismantling the family and segregating its members by age, even for the purpose of targeting special needs, the church fails to equip the family to communicate with one another and live together. But home schooling ideas are getting out into the mainstream. Many churches that have responded to the home-school message are now beginning to pioneer new ways of serving families and letting families serve.

Through the efforts of home schooling families, some churches are also being restored to the original design as age-integrated centers of worship and fellowship. By keeping their children quietly at their side during the regular church services, home-school families are causing a small revolution to take place. For the first time in years, families are being seen together at church. They may part for Sunday school, but they are together in the regular service. Children in such families are much more likely to be integrated into the life of the Body before they are teens. They already enjoy the adult worship service because they have grown up actively involved in it. A Christian family, sitting together and actively involved in worship is a wonderful thing. Home schooling families are bringing this back to the church.

The Value of Age Integration

According to a recent study, home-schooled children are less peer-oriented than children in the conventional private schools.[1] This research suggests that children in the private school "appeared to be more influenced by or concerned with peers than the home educated group."

Because home-schooled children are generally more comfortable in a wider span of age groups, they do not limit their friendships to their age peers. This improves fellowship among the various age groups within the church's children's program. Age integration among children, just as with adults, helps place the focus of social interaction on one's gifts and servanthood, not on seniority.

The blessing of age-integrated education offers additional fruit beyond the church setting. The Christian home-school household's extended family will often include teenagers from other families. This is due to several factors. First of all, the home-school family has more flexible time to include others in its family activities. Second, the home-school family feels the need for adding new members to the family team. It recognizes the practical value of extended family because it is doing more of what a family is intended to do. And when a home-school family reaches out in this way, the individual is received as a friend of the entire family, rather than merely the friend of his age-mate. This relationship helps both the teen's discipleship and the family's home-school program. The family friend gains insight into what a Christian family can be like, and the home-school family gains a helping hand in simple chores and child care.

The Missionary Home School

Most of us have heard stories of bitter missionary children who feel they have been shipped off to boarding school so their parents could minister to others. One example is heard in the bitter cry of this teenager: "I'm a triangle. Do you know what that is? It's a square with something missing. I have always been that way, and always will be. The most anticipated event [for my parents] in my preschool years was when I would get off to school and thus get out of my parents' hair. They then could give their full attention to teaching the natives about the Lord."[2] This is a sad example of the pain children feel when they think God has robbed them of their parents.

Not every missionary child feels this way, but the fact that some do demands that alternatives be found. A growing number of missionary families are recognizing the potential of home schooling to resolve this age-old problem. Home-schooling families can remain together on the mission field and still provide a quality education for each missionary child. In Central American Mission's *Bulletin*, a missionary mother voices the logic of her decision to home school:

> Someone has said, "The home is the unit of society. To this unity God has given responsibility to bring up what it has brought forth. This is God's way—and God's way is the best way." Our main reason for keeping our children at home is that we feel responsible for their training. God gave them to us and we believe we should keep them with us as long as they are children.
>
> How will our children learn secular subjects and spiritual truths? We believe they learn these from the spiritual environment of the home, from direct instruction in the home classes, and from daily associations. The most important lessons our children can learn are learned as they watch us and listen to and take part in the daily conversation of the home.

And the officials of missionary organizations are taking notice. An Overseas Missionary Fellowship booklet notes, "Our leaders have spent perhaps as much time discussing the sticky questions of providing for missionaries' children as for any other subject." And in a recent Wycliffe Bible Translators communication these lines appear:

Wycliffe Bible Translators makes a number of options available in the education of the children of its members. Because each field is democratic and semi-autonomous, these options differ from field to field. But in each case, the Wycliffe member himself decides what plan to follow. If an individual translator does not feel that any plan suggested by the Wycliffe branch is satisfactory, he may choose another course of action for his children.[3]

On further investigation, I was told that home schooling is the fastest growing "other course of action" among Wycliffe missionaries.

Many missionary families feel that the harm caused by the separation of children from their parents outweighs all of the possible benefits of a boarding school, especially when the children are small. It is certainly true that some missionary children have developed problems that can be traced to a traumatic separation from their parents at an early age. But missionary Betty Jo Kenney joyfully reports, "I taught my children five years and treasure the experience. The privilege of sharing so many learning experiences with your child is rare in today's splintered society. If you have this opportunity approach it with positive excitement. Learning can be fun!"[4] Home schooling is a spiritual advantage to the missionary movement.

Home schooling contributes to the spiritual well-being of the child, the family, the neighborhood evangelistic mission, and the church. In the church it reunites families in work, study, instruction, fellowship, worship, and discipleship. And it is also the fastest growing alternative to boarding schools among missionary families. We should not be surprised. Home schooling is part of God's original pattern for the godly family.

Chapter 23, Notes

1. Mona Maarse Delahooke, "Home Educated Children's Social/Emotional Adjustment and Academic Achievement: A Comparative Study (1986)," *Dissertation Abstracts International, 47 (2),* 475A.

2. C. John Buffam, *The Life and Times of an MK* (Pasadena, Calif.: Wm. Carey Library, 1985).

3. From "Who Makes the Decisions in the Education of Missionary Children?" Wycliffe Bible Translators, 77-78. Used by permission.

4. Betty Jo Kenney, *The Missionary Family* (Pasadena, Calif.: Wm. Carey Library, 1983), 56.

CHAPTER 24

Are There Educational Advantages to Home Schooling?

HOME schooling is the best approach to education. It yields better results and it does so in less time and with less money. In a recent study conducted by the Alaska Department of Education, students in outlying areas of this vast northern state were doing better, on average, than their peers in the conventional schools.[1] An earlier survey of home school students reported that their scores on the reading, mathematics, and language portions of the California Achievement Tests (CAT) were on the average 1.04 grades above their actual grade level.[2] Wherever studies of this sort have been conducted, the home-schooled child is demonstrating average to superior ability. How is the home-school family getting these impressive results?

The educational advantages of home schooling are derived primarily from the superiority of tutoring over classroom instruction. A teacher working on a one-on-one basis with a student can make much more progress—in less time and with less stress to the student—than the same teacher in a classroom setting. Tutoring is a better approach to teaching.

The Tutorial Method

Tutoring allows the instructor to focus the student's attention on the studies. In the classroom, the teacher must struggle to maintain the attention of up to thirty children at the same time. In the tutorial setting the same teacher has only one or two students to deal with. Like the circus performer who tries to keep a dozen plates spinning at one time, the classroom instructor must constantly shift his attention from one student to another in a valiant, but hopeless, effort to keep everyone focused on the subject of study.

A tutor in any setting teaches with dialogue rather than monologue. She asks questions about the subject of study which require a thoughtful and understanding response from the student. When the student responds, the tutor picks up on that answer and adds to it a comment or another question. Likewise, the student's questions are taken seriously and responded to in ways that encourage the child to be inquisitive. This dialogue heightens the student's understanding of the subject.

A 1983 study of four-year-olds' questions and adults' answers found that more questions were asked by children at home than in the school program.[3] More disturbing was the evidence that persistent questioning was rare at school, compared to the home: "children seem to learn very quickly that their role at school is to answer, not to ask questions."[4] Additionally the study showed that both adults and children had a wider range and greater complexity of language use at home than at school.

The implication of this study is that if even a typical home is more educational than a school, a home-schooling home will be far superior to a school. Wherever we find the dialogue of tutoring we find better educational progress.

Educational Feedback

A home school tutor keeps the attention of the student through immediate feedback. Using feedback, the tutor can determine immediately whether or not the student really understands what is being discussed and can carefully monitor the subject matter's level of difficulty.

Efficient study requires a proper level of difficulty. A student must be challenged but not frustrated. If the study is not difficult enough, the student becomes bored; if it is too difficult, he becomes frustrated and disillusioned and may turn his attention to something else. Such frustration is often turned inward, and the struggling student begins to blame himself for being "stupid." Early frustration can cripple the student's desire and ability to learn, dooming him to a life of low self-worth and fear of study. The level of difficulty in the growing child's studies must be monitored and adjusted.

In the conventional classroom, the level of difficulty is usually determined by "average ability." Education is geared to the majority. Inevitably, there are children who are bored or frustrated. The "bright" students are waiting for their "slow" classmates to catch up. The "slow" students are wondering why the teacher has to move on so quickly. "Average" students may be comfortable, or they may simply be too quiet to monitor. The "A+" crowd learns how to coast through school without having to apply themselves, and the "D and F" crowd drops out of the race and no longer tries to make it in school. Everybody loses by these classroom comparisons.

Home schools reduce the competition and therefore the need for such comparisons. Each student in the home is simply trying to break new ground in each topic of study. Like a gymnast, he strives to better his own past best, not beat someone else's record. If the work is at the proper level of difficulty, it will nurture in the student a taste for the exhilaration that comes from succeeding at something that does not come easily. The level of feedback needed to make this monitoring possible is not available in large classrooms.

Home schools also have less problem in adapting to the attention span of individual students. When the studies become stressful or tedious, the home-school teacher can turn immediately to another topic, to household chores, or to reading another chapter in whatever book they are reading together. She need not push any child beyond his ability. Individualized instruction allows each student to study at his own pace.

Delight-Directed "Unit" Studies

Many people are skeptical when they hear that home school parents can teach most subjects before lunch time. The report, however, is accurate. Because home schooling mothers are tutoring their children, they are usually able to finish in the morning. That leaves the afternoon free for delight-directed studies.

As mentioned before, Psalm 111:2 tells us, "Great are the works of the LORD, they are pondered by all who delight in them." People, children included, study the things that delight them. If our delight is in the law of the Lord, we will meditate on his law day and night, without coercion (Psalm 1:2). Delight is the biblical basis for study. In the home school we employ this biblical principle by harnessing the wholesome delights of each student and using them to pull the student into areas of study he might never have found interesting as a subject.

Any interest would do, provided it is wholesome and approved by mom and dad. Pets, collections, hobbies, science, sports, and many other delights could support a course of study. Consider, for example, the typical nine-year-old boy's delight in baseball. Even if he doesn't want to study reading, writing, arithmetic, history, science, or American geography, we can watch him make great progress in all of these areas by simply harnessing his delight in sports.

We might begin with a few biographies of baseball greats. The libraries are full of such volumes. As we read to the student, and/or require him to read aloud to us, he stretches his reading skills. A dictionary nearby will be needed, and so will an encyclopedia. As the famous ball player lives through his particular time in history, major events are going to disrupt or further his career. By pausing briefly to look up and explain the nature of these events—be they wars, economic depressions, or technological innovations—we cultivate in the nine-year-old an awareness of the flow of history.

Collecting baseball cards provides an excellent opportunity to work with numbers. Pitching and batting statistics must be tabulated and averaged. Is this math too difficult for a nine-year-old? It might be. But he may amaze you at how quickly he can learn to calculate the things he wants to calculate. He will stretch his skills in written correspondence by requesting an autographed photo of his favorite team. This teaches him the real purpose for neatness, proper grammar, and correct spelling. Following the exploits of various teams across the country opens the door to American geography and map reading. Throwing a curve ball introduces him to physics. Every major physical law comes to bear on that baseball as it curves. Conditioning exercises open to him the world of physical education, anatomy, and nutrition.

If the child is really delighted in baseball, he can even study labor-management negotiations, the history of the civil rights movement, the problem of drug abuse, and the business of professional sports. What a long and elaborate study a simple thing like baseball can become! And all of it is interesting if baseball is what delights you. Such studies cover nearly all the educational bases.

A delight-directed study is not a child-directed study. Good mothers cook what they know their children need, but they prepare it with the individual tastes of each child in mind. They try to make what is good for you also taste good. In the same way, home-school parents prepare delight-directed studies. They know what their child needs next, but they prepare to teach it in terms of what their child is delighted in.

These kinds of afternoon studies are not as practical in the classroom. Not every child will be interested in baseball. The classroom teacher cannot keep every student's delights in view at the same time. The child's understanding of the world begins to come unraveled. His studies of the world around him are seldom delightful, seldom connected to one another or to him in any noticeable way. They have been reduced to subjects.

In the early years of a child's education, the emphasis should be placed on nurturing a taste for the process of study. The content of his study is secondary. Let him study whatever delights him, as long as he really studies it. If we can only instill in him a love for learning, he will devote the rest of his life to study. Great achievers in any field of endeavor have this in common; they love what they do. A great violinist was once told by an admiring fan, "I would give my life to play the violin as well as you do." The musician replied, "I did." This kind of enduring dedication is the result of something deeper than mere professional recognition or financial reward. It is born of delight.

As adults, we read not for reading's sake but for the content available to us through our reading material. We read for a purpose even when we read for pleasure. Conventional schools work against this process by requiring the child to read meaningless or even mindless material. Reading for personal interest and enjoyment is something he must do on his own time. The classroom system of reading instruction makes reading distasteful to too many children and limits the child's development of a lifelong love for reading.

In school, math is often taught as an end in itself, or with the odd promise that "someday you will need this." Someday? What's wrong with today? If we could only give the child a ruler and help him build a birdhouse right in math class, he would recognize the importance of numbers immediately. But in most schools you don't build birdhouses in math class. In math class, you just do math. The child is expected to keep up his motivation to study by sheer willpower or by the fear of failing. He has no reason to delight in numbers. This is not the way to produce great mathematicians.

But should children be expected to study only what they find interesting? Of course not. But the question can be turned around. Should teachers ever teach a subject without attempting to make it as interesting as possible? The chairman of *Encyclopaedia Britannica*, Mortimer J. Adler, has written, "The art of teaching consists in large part of interesting people in things that ought to interest them, but do not. The task of educators is . . . to invent the methods of interesting their students in it."[5]

Is there ever a good reason to do less than we can in nurturing the delight that motivates children to study? If an individualized approach would make the difference between boredom and excitement, is there ever a good reason to deny the child the extra effort? My friends in teaching respond that it is not practical to do so. But I must ask, Where is it impractical? In the classroom? Then let us be honest enough to admit that the classroom is an obstacle to doing our best as teachers. The classroom structure discourages the child from delighting in his studies.

Is Character Taught or Caught?

Probably the greatest educational benefit of home schooling is the character training resulting from the close association of parents with their children. In a close teacher-student relationship, academic content is not the only thing transferred. Character is transferred as well (Luke 6:40; Proverbs 13:20; 1 Corinthians 15:33).

Companionship influences moral discretion. It molds every facet of human personality. But what control do Christian parents have over the character of the public school teachers? The courts have been unanimous on this. The answer is *none*. Yet a teacher's character is of utmost importance. The moral qualities we want to instill in our children have to be present in the one teaching them.

> Mark Hopkins sat on one end of a log
> And a farm boy sat on the other.
> Mark Hopkins came as a pedagogue,
> And taught as an elder brother.
> I don't care what Mark Hopkins taught.
> If his Latin was small and his Greek was naught,
> For the farm boy he thought, thought he,
> All through the lecture time and quiz,
> "The kind of man I mean to be
> Is the kind of a man Mark Hopkins is."[6]

As parents we certainly "care what Mark Hopkins taught." Yet, even more we should care about "what kind of a man Mark Hopkins is," because that, in the long run, will have greater influence on our child.

A Very Special Education

Finally, in the home school the parents of a handicapped child have the opportunity to become the loving teacher-therapists their child needs. Regardless of the challenge that such children pose, godly parents can and do rise (with patience and initiative) to meet the demands. If a child is found to have a learning disability (whether it be minimal brain dysfunction, Down's syndrome, dyslexia, hyperactivity, speech impediment, eye or ear problems, or any other physical or emotional condition), home school parents can, by Christ's power, become specialists in serving their child's unique needs. At home, the child's diet and medication can be better regulated. He is able to relax and learn away from the confusing demands of a school setting.

A child's serious handicap usually brings out a wealth of devotion and dedication in parents. Not that it is easy—it is an adventure in parenting which has its casualties as well as its success stories. But loving parents who delight in their child will study to become whatever the child needs them to be. Doing so requires parents to seek out a multitude of counselors and learning specialists who are willing to share what they know with the parents. Out-of-home programs can supplement what parents are doing in the home. And the needs of other children may require day-care for the handicapped child during certain periods of time each week. Home schooling encourages and facilitates this creative response to a common dilemma, and many medical centers across the U.S. are expressing excitement over the results these parents are enjoying.

All of the advantages of the home described previously become so much more important when the child is struggling with a learning disability. Tutoring becomes necessary rather than optional, and the child's love for learning is crucial because he will have to apply himself much more persistently than other children. The social stigma often caused by special education classes is not a threat in the home school. The home provides a practical alternative to institutional school programs.

Yes, But What About . . . ?

In spite of all these educational advantages, some people still have sincere doubts about the viability of home schooling. They harbor questions they assume home schoolers could never answer, and so out of kindness they do not ask. Rest assured we have heard every question. In fact we asked them ourselves before we made our decision to teach at home.

In these cases I find it helpful to expose the absurdity of these questions by applying them to another sacred aspect of family life—home cooking. I am convinced that every argument framed against home schooling can just as easily be directed against home cooking. It just sounds silly when you do.

"Home cooking could be a harbor for dietary neglect."

"Our children are too valuable a national resource to be left to amateur cooks. After all, You are what you eat."

"You should not be allowed to cook at home unless you are a certified nutritionist."

"Home kitchen equipment cannot be adequate."

"All children should be required to eat three standardized meals a day in government-operated cafeterias."

"I've had a few home-cooked meals that were abusive."

"Children need to eat around other children in order to learn proper table manners."

"Children need to eat in restaurants in order to experience all the varieties of ethnic cooking."

"I could never cook for my children every day. So I send them to the local restaurants. They're professionals."

"If everybody cooked at home, the restaurants would have to close and millions of people would starve."

"I know someone who is a terrible cook."

Have I missed any? Home schooling is not afraid of questions. If you have what you think is the killer question, ask it. The odds are we've heard it many times before. And if that question is all that is standing between you and home schooling, we will be glad to help you get it out of the way.

In summary, most of the educational advantages of the home relate to the efficiency and effectiveness of tutoring. The low student-teacher ratio allows for more individualized instruction, more immediate educational feedback, more delight-directed studies which target the wholesome interests of the student, and better monitoring of the level of difficulty in each student's instruction. All of these advantages are especially valuable when the child has a learning disability to overcome. With a multitude of counselors and the right amount of personal initiative, parents can become the instructor-therapists their children need. Like home cooking, home schooling is as wholesome and natural as "mom and apple pie."

Chapter 24, Notes
1. "Results from 1981 CAT [Centralized Correspondence Study]" (Juneau, Alaska: Alaska Department of Education, 1986).
2. Norma J. F. Linden, in "Investigation of Alternative Education: Home Schooling (1983)," *Dissertation Abstracts International, 44,* 3457A.
3. B. Tizard, M. Hughes, H. Caramchel, and G. Pinkerton, "Children's Questions and Adults' Answers," *Journal of Child Psychology and Psychiatry* 24:269-81.
4. Ibid., 279.
5. Mortimer J. Adler, *Great Books of the Western World,* vol. 1, *The Great Conversation,* 49.
6. Arthur Gutterman, as quoted in Gaines S. Dobbins, *Great Teachers Make A Difference* (Nashville: Broadman Press, 1965), 22.

CHAPTER 25

How Will Our Child Benefit Socially from Home Schooling?

B Y far the most common question asked of home educators is, "How are your kids going to learn to get along with others if they never get to be with other children their own age? They won't be able to fit into the real world if you don't let them experience life outside the four walls of your home." Questions like this imply that home schooling parents never think about this dimension of their child's training.

In reality, effective social training is one of the primary reasons for home schooling. Studies show that home schooling parents spend as much or more time developing the social graces of their children than parents using conventional schools do.[1] The opportunity to put extra time and effort into socialization is one of the strengths of home schooling.

People of good will want to know how home schoolers intend to rear children who will be comfortable and skillful in society when parents can no longer be there to protect them. This is a reasonable concern, and we have several responses. But first we must define the terms and the goals of socialization.

The Nature of Identity

Human beings are social creatures who need times of social interaction. This is because our sense of identity is made up of all our most significant relationships in life. Ask anyone to tell you in detail who he is, and he will list his important relationships: marriage, children, church affiliation, nationality, work, and friends. A self-concept is the sum of these relationships.

This is not the same as identity based on performance or acceptance by others. People who are driven to perform and accomplish in order to feel like they are somebody have fallen for Satan's lie—you have to do good to be accepted by God (Galatians 3:11). By God's grace, we are already somebody. By divine creation, we bear the image of God. But in the scheme of God's design, we are placed into a unique set of relationships with other persons, places, and things. We can look around, therefore, and see where we are and know where we fit into God's plan. This becomes our working definition of who we are, and it is an important part of our emotional and spiritual health.

People are distinguished by more than politics, race, doctrine, law, and economics. They are differentiated by gender, age, experience, and moral character. People are designed by God to make personal progress over a period of time. We call this growing up. A child is not only supposed to grow bigger, he is intended to become better in many ways. The path of life is to be an upward journey toward higher and higher levels of wisdom, skill, and maturity. Some are ahead of others in this journey.

Because of this, age, experience, and character differences are important elements in a child's sense of identity. His sense of progress toward maturity, in relationship to others, is artificially raised or lowered by his experience in an age- and maturity-segregated setting.

This is why home schoolers believe that social training outside of an age- and maturity-integrated setting has limited usefulness. It distorts the real world as God established it. If a child no longer reaches toward the maturity of his parents or older siblings, his orientation becomes horizontal. He becomes peer-oriented, and eventually, peer-dependent. He stops trying to grow up because growing up is no longer what it takes to be popular. On the contrary, trying to grow up may be disastrous to your social status in a school.

God places children, even when they seem to arrive in litters, in a basically age-integrated family. Parents are always older than their own children and the natural extended family brings together a wider span of ages. When several children are born over a period of time and the family practices a healthy routine of hospitality, everyone enjoys the full scope of life's relationships. The child must answer to those who are older and wiser. He is also responsible for those who are younger or weaker. This is the setting in which the growing child can best learn the skills of social interaction; this is the real world. Age segregation, as found in conventional classrooms, is an artificial contrivance. It is the product of school administration.

Everything Is Looking Up

In the natural age-integrated setting everything points the child toward higher levels of maturity. The structure of family relationships encourages the child to do the things his older brothers and sisters are doing. He wants to learn to do whatever others are doing. He is impatient. He wants to grow up now. Small children often remark that they are a "big boy" or "big girl." They delight in showing others what they can do "all by themselves." It is obvious that the goal of their lives is to be like the older and wiser members of their family. So the family, as a social laboratory, is working.

But the family is not the whole world. Proper participation in the weekly services and fellowship of a local church enrich the experience of the home school child. Neighborhood friendships further adorn the fabric of his early social life. Yet these contexts remain basically age-integrated. Only in the new "Adults Only" apartment complexes and the increasingly age-stratified fellowship activities of some churches do we see the pattern broken. Perhaps these are early warnings of what the effects of age segregation in our society will be.

The Hurried Child

Children's clubs, scouting, and sports can add to a child's social life. The fear that a child is being deprived of social contacts is normally unwarranted. On the contrary, childhood has become a menagerie of too many things to do and join. Far from being isolated, children are often stressed emotionally by the overwhelming number of social activities. Dr. David Elkind has made an excellent case for slowing down this parade of socialization in his book *The Hurried Child*.[2] He observes that for the vast majority of children, the problem is not a lack of social contacts, it is an over abundance of age-segregated group contacts. Children are being burned out. They spend too much time with other children.

Age Segregation and Peer Dependency

In 1 Kings 12 we have a remarkable story about a young king named Rehoboam, who suffered the consequences of age segregation and peer dependency. Soon after his coronation, he was implored by his people to lower the taxes and other burdens placed on the people by his father, King Solomon. The young king realized the decision was an important test of his ability and so he sent the people away for three days while he consulted with his counselors.

The elders who had served his father Solomon advised him to yield to the people's request in order to establish his throne in good will. But Rehoboam wanted more counsel. He turned to the young men who had been his friends in childhood and asked them what he should do. They advised him to be tough and to increase the taxes immediately just to show Israel who's boss. Rehoboam rejected the advice of the elders and followed the advice of his childhood friends. As a result, the people rebelled, and the kingdom was torn in two.

Rehoboam's father, King Solomon had written, "He who walks with the wise grows wise, but a companion of fools suffers harm" (Proverbs 13:20). It appears as though Rehoboam spent too much time in the company of fools.

Solomon's proverb is a promise and a warning about the power of companionship. It should cause us to reevaluate our own social life. Who have we been spending our time with? Are they wise? The Bible suggests that age and wisdom go together, and that children, because of their stubbornness and inexperience, can be very foolish (Proverbs 22:15). This biblical principle has serious implications for the prevalence of age-segregated instruction in our schools. Classroom instruction is leading to peer orientation among students, even in the Christian schools. Negative companionship is destroying our youth.

Age-segregated classrooms are harmful to children because children, more than anyone else, need to know their identity. They are looking for their place in this world. If taken out of the natural setting of their home for too much of the time, children are forced to collect a new set of peer group relationships to provide a new sense of identity in the new setting. They begin to search for friends. This shows up in the drive to be popular.

Children lack social skills, experience, or discretion in selecting their companions. Appearances often take center stage. The prettiest, the strongest, and the most stylish rule. The mouthiest, the most ruthless, the most rebellious climb the pecking order to become leaders and opinion makers in the developing classroom culture. And these things begin to happen in the first few grades.

Any child and family counselor can recount the emotional damage inflicted on children by their age-mates in school. Being picked last for the kickball team can cause a child to see himself as "undesirable." To be called "fatty" or "ugly" in front of everyone can destroy a child's self-image and cripple his confidence for years. Children are the victims of one another's foolish and insensitive behavior. But there is another, more dreadful kind of harm caused by foolish companions. Children can be corrupted.

Paul admonishes us, "Do not be misled: 'Bad company corrupts good character'" (1 Corinthians 15:33). Corruption of character is the ultimate harm that comes to the companion of fools. And because of it this world will one day end (Colossians 3:5-6). Parental standards are quickly discarded, seemingly without thought, as soon as the approval of a child's peers gains greater importance to him than the approval of his parents.

Age-segregated companionship is finally being recognized for the hazard it is. Dr. Fred Beauvais of Colorado State University reports that "friends" in school are five times more influential in a teenager's decision to abuse drugs than any other lifestyle factor. Parents are not even in the running. Harm is showing up in the form of disregard for authority, preteen sex, drug abuse, theft, vandalism, violence, and suicide. Paul tells us to "have nothing to do" with those who promote a godless lifestyle (2 Timothy 3:1-5). There is a time when we have to distance ourselves from the corrupting influences of this world and strengthen the things which remain.

Our children long for companionship and continue to seek it among age-mates who cannot maintain a stable relationship. Too often they end up tossing parental values overboard to satisfy their desire to belong. What is the solution?

We can only hope to solve this growing crisis by first teaching our own children faithfully and then by including other children in our home school as the opportunity arises.[3] God would have us begin with our own children. We must let them walk with the two wise Christian companions God assigned to them from the womb. That companionship, along with biblical hospitality, is the best socialization.

The Alternative: Open Heart, Open Home

"In a matter of weeks he was like a new boy. He is so much more cheerful and relaxed. It's amazing!" That is the common report I receive from parents who have taken their children out of school and started teaching them at home. The stressful tempest is left behind, and eventually the sound of the storm begins to fade. Fear of what other children will think is gone. Respect for mom and dad return. The child comes back to his old (more pleasant) self again.

The home is the best place for teaching social skills. It is a place of security for the child. When parents make the effort, it provides an atmosphere where the child is confident enough to develop new skills and to try new approaches to getting along with others. Mutual respect is the foundation for this atmosphere.

Conflict resolution is much easier to learn at home. There is usually no lack of conflict to practice on. Wherever there are two people there is potential for crossed purposes. But at home a child can "give in" and forgive others with less fear of being taken advantage of. The home allows the child to practice specifically coached skills, such as argumentation, salesmanship, and mediation. It also allows for the slow and natural development of living skills. For instance, conversation skills must be developed by the combination of example, instruction, practice, gentle correction, and encouragement. It takes time. Common courtesy and table manners are likewise the result of many small but intentional sessions sprinkled throughout the routine of daily living. Imagine trying to teach these graces in the average school cafeteria.

And remember, all these high-level social skills will be needed long before the child grows up and leaves the home school. First are those guest audiences from the neighborhood who come for dessert and stay for a school presentation. Then there are the support group activities. Children work together on group projects that sometimes take weeks or months to complete. Good friends are made during these times. A few good friends, known and approved by the parents, are more precious than a thousand acquaintances.

For more adventure, the home-school family can have many national and international friendships. Developing these friendships requires a little initiative, but it can be done by any family willing to reach out to traveling missionaries and foreign students. And home-school families make special use of these international occasions to study the appropriate history, geography, and language of each guest before he arrives.

Families who practice this kind of educational hospitality are also likely to invite skilled musicians, artists, mathematicians, and writers into their home. Talented people will usually be delighted to meet a home-school child, especially if that child has expressed an interest in the guest's special field of endeavor. A violin piece played for your children in your own living room by a member of your local symphony is the best way I know to introduce fine music. Later, when you take your children to see their new-found friend perform in public, they will watch and listen with an entirely new depth of appreciation. This is "touching the palate" of the child, through the power of companionship, and it is the best kind of social training.

The caricature of the isolated home-school child starved for friendships and socially stunted is absurd. Home schoolers have discovered the joy of sharing their home with others. For every one example of social isolation, I can point to a hundred children who are more socially skilled than the average adult, and usually more interesting to talk with as well. Social skills are not developed by the trial-and-error approach of an age-segregated classroom. They are the result of intentional training in the real world of age-integrated family life.

The Results of Our Own Socialization

Some parents believe it's impractical to keep their children home from school. It's difficult for them to imagine how they could ever include children in their daily routine, practice hospitality, and provide academic training across the kitchen table. Schools seem so convenient. They seem so natural to us because we went there as children. But the schools are not good for children, and they are getting worse.

But even if the schools were a good thing, what do non-home schooling parents do during summer vacations? Do they find some way to include their children during the summertime? I certainly hope so. And if it's practical to be together as a family when school lets out, why is it considered impractical to remain a family all year round? The problem is not with having enough time. It is with making the right choices with the time we have.

"By wisdom a house is built, and through understanding it is established; through knowledge its rooms are filled with rare and beautiful treasures" (Proverbs 24:3). Wisdom is the ability to see everything from God's point of view. It gives us perspective, allowing us to see how all things relate—in this case, how child training relates to everything else God has called us to do. God gives wisdom to those who ask for it. But it is proven in the heat of daily living.

Perhaps the reason so many of us today cannot imagine a lifestyle where all of God's revealed will fits neatly together into one family routine is that so few of us have been allowed to walk with wise "elders" who have done it or who are doing it. We are products of our own socialization process, graduates of the public schools. We feel incompetent. We believe the experts. We worry about what others might think. And we pool our inexperience to decide what sounds practical. If we don't take a stand, where will it end?

If we make wisdom our goal, our lives will become visual aids in teaching our children how to be wise as well. They will walk with the wise. Our home will be their best school for social skills and every other facet of the godly life. By our companionship we will be our child's best and most influential teachers. And someday, if we do it right, others will come to us for advice.

Chapter 25, Notes

1. Gunnar A. Gustavsen, "Selected Characteristics of Home Schools and Parents Who Operate Them (1981)," *Dissertation Abstracts International, 42 (10)*, 4381A, 4382A. Gustavsen found in his study of the characteristics of home-schooling families that 64 percent regularly attended religious services. In addition to church activities, the parents participated in no fewer social activities than average. Because most home-schooling families in this study (53 percent) resided in rural or small town situations, we can assume that maintaining an average outside social life is a matter of intentional effort.

2. David Elkind, *The Hurried Child: Growing Up Too Fast Too Soon* (Reading, Mass.: Addison-Wesley Publishing Co., 1981).

3. A seminar conducted by Margaret Skutch explains how home-schooling families can provide "early learning centers" for neighbor children. Her program could provide a partial solution to the dilemma of single parents who desire to provide home-based education for their children in the early years. For more information write to Margaret Skutch, c/o Christian Life Workshops, 180 S.E. Kane Road, Gresham, OR 97080.

CHAPTER 26

How Will Our Family Benefit from Home Schooling Our Child?

"**H**OW do I do it?" asked Millie. "Soccer practice, then the school play rehearsal, and then the evening youth meeting at the church. Drive, drive, drive is all I seem to be doing these days. I feel like Millie's Taxi Service. My kids keep me running here and there all day. And Bob's work doesn't allow any time for him to see the kids. How's a parent supposed to maintain any semblance of family life?"

It's true, today's fast lane living keeps the family on the run and allows little time for family togetherness. Home schooling can help families find balance. Parents and their children can be knit together rather than torn apart. While conventional schools attempt to take the place of the parents[1], home schooling encourages parents to be restored to their strategic place in the lives of their children. The home-schooling parent does not forfeit his position in his child's life, instead he capitalizes on it.

As stated earlier, the home school integrates the responsibilities of the household with the educational goals of each family member. Every adventure of the Christian household provides a lab class for the home-school student. Experience may not always be the best teacher, but without experience our ideas can become theoretical and unrealistic. As the U.S. Department of Education has stated, "Cause and effect are not always obvious, and it may take an experiment to make that clear. Experiments help children actually see how the natural world works."[2] By involving children in the real-life adventure of family living, home-schooling parents are using the most advanced educational techniques of the day. We are learning by doing. And in so doing, we are getting the benefit as a family. Christian homes need to be involved in several adventures in order to have all the necessary lab courses.

Family Business

Business is a broad term. Paul tells us in 1 Thessalonians 4:11-12 to, "Make it your ambition to lead a quiet life, to mind your own business and to work with your hands, just as we told you, so that your daily life may win the respect of outsiders and so that you will not be dependent on anybody." Enterprising, or businesslike, stewardship draws the family together to provide for the household. The family's business interests begin with home economics. Frugality and wisdom in how we spend the money we have is the first step toward having something left over to invest in a small family venture. As each member of the family participates in the family business, they begin to understand what a necessary part of a team they play. The family, not just dad and mom, are earning the household's living. The possible combination of graphic arts, accounting, project management, market research, salesmanship, secretarial work, not to mention the skills directly related to the business's product or service, will create a delight-directed study for the entire family.

At the high school level it is not uncommon for home-schooling families to form an educational co-op or family business club to address this adventure with greater financial resources. A home school version of Junior Achievement can be organized by just a few families. Meetings can focus on every facet of home and family business management. Membership fees can create a small fund for maintaining a loan library of books and tapes on Christian business principles. The small companies started by teens with this kind of support and encouragement are then able to provide money for college education and other needs. My own teenage son, Josh, pays for half of his gymnastics and piano fees out of the profits his business activity generates.

Guest Room Hospitality

Hospitality can be the simple sharing of meals with friends and neighbors. That is a good place to start. But home-schooling families have discovered the adventure of offering guest accommodations to international students, visiting missionaries, and traveling Christians. Practicing hospitality provides an endless flow of friendships and memories for the family to hold in common.

We launch the adventure of guest room hospitality by simply putting our address and phone number in our denomination's ministry magazine as a home open to hosting missionaries and pastors. When guests arrive, our home-schooling students will have questions to ask, presentations to give, and instruction to receive from our guests. The combination works well. Home-school students have a greater personal interest in those nations where they have established friendships. Later the friendships mature into invitations to travel around the world. And if the student has been diligent in his business activities, he will have the means to accept these invitations. Again my own son, Josh, paid for two-thirds of his expenses in traveling to Sapporo, Japan. It was quite an adventure for one so young. But now his friendship with his Japanese hosts is a precious possession.

Civil Influence

Civil influence introduces children to the responsibilities of citizenship. A family's participation in anti-abortion demonstrations or involvement in obtaining sufficient signatures to put a candidate on the ballot can give the children a sense of importance. They learn that their efforts do make a difference. Families can also volunteer to work at local political party headquarters. This introduces children to the functions of our republic, while allowing us to serve together as a family.

A small group of home-schooling teens can be given the assignment to pick a problem in the community and implement a strategy to solve it. It may be a building that needs to be restored with community support, or an intersection that needs a stop sign, or a park that has need of new and less dangerous playground equipment. Any of these can be made an issue as the teens write letters, request interviews, raise funds and otherwise demonstrate their concerns to the community. In a sense, the home-school child can be given the assignment to make history in our community. In this way we can involve the next generation in the social and political processes that make things happen, even before they are old enough to vote.

Adventures in Being Together

All of these household adventures require delight-directed study. The home school is open to every member as each discovers his or her own need for continuing education. How do you go into business? What are the tax codes? What is the form of government in New Zealand? Where do you file your petitions? All these activities demand study, and real-life situations create the best environment for learning. Family business studies in banking, math, accounting, nutrition, and financial policy make for a natural curriculum.

The family who has never home schooled is likely to wonder how a family could ever find the time for so many adventures in learning and ministry. The answer is that the home-schooling family is freed from the bondage of regular schooling hours. The home-school household can redesign its daily routine to meet its own interests rather than the convenience of the local school district.

There is no school bus to catch; no car pool to connect with. The home-school child can rise and retire at whatever hours best fit the family's schedule. No longer bound by a power outside the home, the family can be creative in the organizing of work, study, and recreation.

Extracurricular activities such as sports, drama, ballet, piano lessons, scouting, and various hobby-related clubs round out an education. But all of these things take time. When in addition to these activities the child is enrolled in a conventional school for six or more hours per day, the routine is far too stressful. Conventional school parents often complain of exhaustion. Their lives are a frantic race to meet each child's schedule of activities. In the home-school lifestyle the schedule is more relaxed and these activities can be accommodated in a way that is healthy for the student and his family.

Learning As You Go

Home-schooling families are free to travel. They can take a trip across town or across the country, as the need or the desire arises. No more waiting for the kids to get out for a summer vacation that lasts too long and is all lumped together during the height of the tourist season. The home school can hold school for ten to twelve weeks at a time and then have a nice week or two for travel or special projects. They avoid the crowds at the Grand Canyon and at Yellowstone by visiting with their children during the slower seasons. They can visit the museums and science centers during regular school hours. That is freedom from the school's clock.

Children Totally Involved in Family Life

Home schooling gives parents the opportunity to include children in the necessary routine of the family. Life has its rhythm. We can use that rhythm to teach (Deuteronomy 6:7). Instead of striving to be popular, the home-school child is striving to be a skillful host to a missionary family from France. Rather than selling candy for Junior Achievement, home-school kids are making decisions on how to reinvest the profits they made last month on their family's lawn care business. Rather than skipping school to hang out at another student's home while his parents are away, the home-schooling student is taking the day off to go hiking with his dad and a few home-school support group families. Instead of trying to get a cute cheerleader elected to the student council, they are helping their parents get a prolife candidate elected mayor of the city. These patterns of family life, made possible by home schooling, are good for the entire family.

Do You Know Where Your Kids Are?

When I was growing up, the television announcer would say every night, "It's eleven o'clock. Do you know where your children are?" We would all say, "We're right here," and our parents would laugh. I shudder to think what the answer to that question might be for so many families today. The stakes are so much higher: sexually-transmitted diseases are incurable, drugs are so much more inexpensive and addictive, violence is so much more lethal. And eleven o'clock is no longer the only hour to be concerned.

Many a public-school parent has been shocked to find out, much too late, what has been going on in school during regular hours. Student safety is a critical concern. Violence in the halls and school grounds is a national disgrace. "Statistics, backed by scores of national investigations, indicate junior and senior high schools are riddled by drug abuse and student violence to the degree that teaching and learning have been replaced by the effort just to survive."[3]

This does not mean the public schools have nothing at all to contribute. They are obviously the best option some families have, but they are not an option to be preferred if you have an alternative. Until the church is able and willing to step into the educational gap with a strong private system of home schools and campus schools, I am in favor of continuing the public school system. In fact I urge Christians to consider service in the public schools as a form of missionary work in preparation for change. But we should never encourage parents to send their children to these institutions as they now exist if other alternatives are available.

Home schooling does allow you to know where your kids are, every hour of the day. They are involved in wholesome, real-life activities. They're studying and growing. They're even changing their world for the better. They're taking their first steps toward financial independence and reaching out for the first time to the world beyond our shores. That's where they are. They're at home. And that is very good for the family.

Chapter 26, Notes

1. Susan Douglas Franzosa, "The Wisest and Best Parent: A Critique of John Holt's Philosophy of Education," *Urban Education*, October 1984, 227-44.
2. *What Works: Research About Teaching and Learning* (Washington, D.C.: U. S. Department of Education, 1986), 23.
3. David H. Paynter, *Must Our Schools Die?* (Portland, Ore.: Multnomah Press, 1980), 81.

CHAPTER 27

How Does Home School Education Help Society?

A recent study by the U.S. Department of Education showed that our public-school system is falling behind most other industrialized nations in academic excellence. In a fourteen-nation study, the United States ranked twelfth in proficiency of teaching eighth grade math, sixteen percentage points behind the leader, Japan.[1] In that same study we came in last in ability to teach twelfth graders algebra and calculus.

Fewer young adults enjoy reading today. We have an abundance of functionally illiterate high school graduates. Math and science students are discouraged by the current approach. Our conventional schools are failing to stimulate proper intellectual and spiritual appetites in our young. We are drifting farther away from national greatness, and we seem to be helpless in doing anything about it.

For any society to survive, there must be an uninterrupted flow of competent leaders. Pastors, businessmen, engineers, artists, scientists, and military leaders are crucial to our continued freedom. The thin veneer of our civilization is only about eighteen years deep. Let one generation slip by without receiving the accumulated heritage and technology of its nation and that nation is ended. We have such a short time to instill knowledge and virtue in our youth.

Unfortunately, the family has become passive. For the most part, families do not feel responsible to solve the educational problems of their own students. Instead families expect some other institution of government or business or religion to intervene. Even those few who are concerned "are unsure of what to do or how to do it."[2] This apathy and confusion, in combination with the small birth rates of the last two decades, will surely result in a dearth of qualified professionals in the next few years. We will suffer for the carelessness and shortsightedness of this period of history.

What is worse, many parents act as if they are helpless to stop unprincipled men from seducing and recruiting their children. Evil men in the music and entertainment industries are marketing utter foolishness to children. Perversion, New-Age pop psychology, and materialism bombard us. If we refuse to be the faithful gatekeepers of the media our children consume, we will pay dearly. Greedy businessmen, lacking all principle, want to touch our children's palates with their advertising, instilling in them tastes and appetites for unnecessary goods and services. Licentious "liberation" movements want to recruit our children as well. They think they can change the world without changing the hearts of men. These enemies want to steal our arrows and aim them at their foolish targets. If we allow them to succeed, we will surely be wounded by the members of our own households.

Though home schooling does not provide a massive solution to the schooling crisis, or any other crisis, it offers a practical personal solution. For those families who teach their children at home, the results are rewarding. Word is getting out. Home schooling works for the family. That is why a growing number of Christian parents are saying to school officials, "You've had your chance. Your theories have failed. The lives of our children, the future of the church, and the future of our society are at stake. We are taking charge of our child's education again."

A Sharper Arrow

In the academic sphere alone, the benefits and advantages of home schooling children are impressive. In those cases where standardized testing has been administered to large groups of students, the home-school student is doing quite well. The arrow is being sharpened most effectively.

For example, the Washington State Superintendent of Public Instruction found in 1985 that the majority of Standard Achievement Test (SAT) scores for children K-8 in the "parent as tutor" program "were average, or above average, in Reading, Language and Math." Similar test results in Alaska showed that the home-schooling students did better, much better, than students in the conventional schools.

A Well-Aimed Arrow

Additionally, one recent study verifies the claim of many home schoolers that their children are developing stronger self-concepts and more secure identities. This study compared the self-concept of home-school students with those of students in conventional schools. The findings were encouraging. The self-concept of home-school youth was significantly higher than that of conventional-school youth. On the global scale, half of the home schoolers scored at or above the ninety-first percentile. "Insofar as self-concept is a reflector of socialization . . .

the findings of this study would suggest that few home-schooling children are socially deprived."[3] If our goal is to see our children remain true to their training, self-concept is likely to be a deciding factor.

Home Schooling is Cost Effective

The home school is also more cost effective than any other option in education. I will address the financial advantages of home education in detail in the next chapter, but the home school utilizes household facilities and resources already accumulated for the larger good of the home. This efficient use of the home for education reduces the burden on the state and the church, allowing these jurisdictions to focus their attention on those children whose parents are unable or unwilling to provide education in their homes.

Obviously some form of conventional school will always be necessary for many children, just as orphanages will always be necessary for children who have no parents. But to require all children to participate in the programs designed for orphans is both expensive and unnecessary. Our social "safety nets" are not to become hammocks for negligent parents. It is much more prudent to strengthen the hands of responsible parents and then devote state and church resources only to those children who need their services.

Home-School Graduates Make Good Leaders

People who are able to deal with society from a position of personal strength rather than weakness will be better able to guide the affairs of their families, their churches, and their nation. Studies in the public school community show that leadership ability is best developed in the smaller schools. Rural schools of three hundred students or less provide many more leadership opportunities for each student than the larger urban or suburban schools. Logically, the more personal and intimate the social groups in which a student participates, the more often the student will be required to think for himself and initiate leadership. Home-schooling support groups, age-integrated as they are, provide such experience.

Home Schooling Provides a Superior Foundation for International Friendship and Understanding

What can one family do for world peace? On the home school front, international friendship can be established through guest room hospitality. People and events go hand in hand, and the hospitality of one family can change the course of a nation's history. A home-school family in Austin, Texas, had opportunity to receive a young foreign student from Communist China. After several visits and a great deal of ministry, this young man was discovered to be a popular film and music personality in his country. The friendship continues and many are praying that God will use this young man to open the hearts of Chinese youth to the gospel.

It is good to have personal contacts in other countries around the world. In this way, students can be made aware of the accuracy or distortion of events as reported by the news media. In my own home, we had the opportunity to entertain an overnight guest from South Africa. This dear friend's explanation of his country's crisis was insightful. My teenage son now has a friend whose account of his nation's history gives current events new meaning. In this case, our international hospitality has induced a healthy skepticism toward the media. Greater political discretion has been born. This allows my family to be more independent in their thinking concerning various issues facing our society.

Home Schooling Develops Independent Thinkers

Independent thinking is never an absolute value. The need for advice and counsel exists for all of us

(Proverbs 11:14; 15:22; 24:6). The home school is able to develop a leadership mentality that is still responsive to wise counsel. Rather than walking in the counsel of inexperienced age-mates, the home-school student is more likely to seek out the opinion of those older and more experienced than himself. This prepares him to participate in the real world of age- and maturity-integrated society.

In business, in ministry, in social and civil movements, and in the management of his own household, the student will be confronted with hierarchies of age, skill, and experience. By relating to these on a smaller scale within his family, he is more likely to be able to relate to seniority structures as an adult.

Home-schooled teenagers are often much more comfortable around adults than their counterparts in the conventional schools. Their willingness to be responsible to those older than themselves and responsible for those younger than themselves is confirmed by many in their churches and communities. The fruit of home schooling is sweet.

The Gathering Storms

The sanctity of human life. The benefit to society of this type of youngster is of special importance in the light of the gathering support for euthanasia and infanticide in our country. Surgeon General C. Everett Koop has warned that by the year 2005, we could face ten thousand cases of death by euthanasia or medicated suicide for every one infanticide case in the 1980s.

It is frightening to consider the consequences of raising up another generation that has so little sense of responsibility toward the elderly. If civil laws related to the sanctity of human life are further eroded, and if liberal propagandists continue to encourage society to accept euthanasia and medicated suicide as a legitimate means of avoiding pain, loneliness, and medical expense, we could expect a slaughter far beyond any racial extermination known in the past.

AIDS. With the rise of the AIDS epidemic, it would not be surprising to see the victims of this terrible disease, infants as well as adults, manipulated into receiving or volunteering for "early relief" by means of active euthanasia. Already we hear voices advocating suicide as a solution to AIDS. This storm alone will drastically change the course of the next ten years. Life will not go on as usual.

The solution to this problem will not be found exclusively through the home-school movement. Again, we have to view home schooling as a personal solution. The home-school family can choose not to be part of the problem and thereby be able to work toward a more far-reaching solution. By God's grace, the Christian home-school family will do what it can to lead our nation toward the renewal of the sanctity of all human life.

Racial unrest. In the last few decades, valiant attempts have been made through the public school and other government agencies to integrate the races of American society. The consequences of their attempts have been as mixed as the approaches. Racial tension continues to be a problem in the urban community, Americans still flee from contact with other races, frustrating the attempts of government to knit together the fabric of our society.

The legal and economic aspects of racial discrimination require government intervention in some cases. Liberty and justice must be for all. However, laws cannot create friendships. Certain aspects of community have at their base a spiritual dimension.

The home school, in cooperation with the Christian school, is able to address this spiritual dimension in a way that the public school by nature cannot. In some cases, the public schools' impotence in the face of vandalism, drug abuse, and violence heightens the racial tensions. They create an environment where children meet children of other races on a battleground. Fear and revenge derail what may have been friendships in any other setting.

In contrast to this, the Christian home school has shown that it can reach across racial boundaries and encourage true fellowship and community among families and children from various ethnic groups. The fact that these contacts are often cross-generational as well as interracial strengthens our hope that the body of Christ can lead the way in producing examples of brotherhood to our nation.

There are in our ranks a handful of racists, just as there are in every other segment of our society. The ability of these groups and individuals to capture media attention by their outrageous statements tells us more about the competence of the news media than it does about home schooling. But for the good of society, home schooling must always be an honored and encouraged option in education. It is a freedom deserved by those parents who have the initiative and self-discipline to embrace it.

Our Vision

Consider for a moment the high vision that motivates so many Christian home school families. This is the gift we hope to give to our society for the glory of our Lord Jesus Christ and the good of all men. Our gift will be our children. We are not deterministic. We realize there are no guarantees or formulas for success in child training. The nature of the child will be affected by the nurture of the home, but our hope is in God. Therefore, we know our labor in the Lord is not in vain.

Our hope and strategy is that the unique advantages of our home schools will produce a generation of children who will serve our society from a position of moral strength. Rather than struggling with a weak sense of identity, the ideal home-schooled child will have a quietness and confidence that projects godly strength. Our objective is that each child learn from his own parents how to meet the world with a biblical agenda and how to use every opportunity God gives him to achieve goals he has chosen for himself in the light of God's Word.

In the process of pursuing this vision we are giving a second gift as well. We are trying to lead our children by the power of our own example. We are taking care of our own businesses and providing for our own households so that our home-school graduates will too. Our homes are more of a blessing to society than they would have been otherwise. As each home-school graduate steps out of his father's house to establish a household of his own, we want him to have faithful and realistic strategies. If he has learned them for himself through years of close involvement in his own family's life, he will prosper and so will the community around him.

In our vision, the ideal home-schooled student, with a family of his own, will show himself to be a faithful member of his church, a provider for his own household, a blessing to his neighbor, a business person of integrity, and a citizen of loyalty. It is a high vision, but one we can gladly spend our lives to fulfill.

Chapter 27, Notes

1. "Second International Mathematics Study" (Washington, D.C.: U.S. Department of Education, National Center for Education Statistics, 1985).

2. *What Works: Research About Teaching and Learning* (Washington, D.C.: U.S. Department of Education, 1986), 19.

3. John Wesley Taylor, "Self-Concept of Home Schooling Children," *Home School Researcher*, June 1986, 1.

CHAPTER 28

What Do I Need to Know about Financing a Home School?

CHRISTIAN education is much more than a business transaction; it is a ministry. The spiritual and emotional dimensions of school and family make a dollars-and-cents discussion seem out of place. But like most other things in this world, profit and loss are factors to be considered. Every school, even the public school, must face the pressures of a free market society. Schools must either compete well or disband.

Some will always patronize the public schools merely because they provide a free education. In my discussion of the financial advantages of home schooling, I choose to dismiss public schooling on the grounds that it is not the quality of schooling I want to buy. Buying shoes on sale is no advantage if the size or the color is not what is needed. Therefore, no matter how inexpensive public schooling may be, it is not the education I want for my children. Bargain or no bargain, I'm shopping elsewhere.

That narrows my choices to local Christian schools or my own home school. The comparison between these is the primary focus of my presentation in "The Home Schooling Workshop." On the financial level, home schooling, like home cooking, can seem like "unfair" competition. Moms don't charge for their services as teachers, and so the overhead expenses of the home school are much lower. The home can prepare and serve a higher quality lesson for less money. The requisite knowledge, skills, and equipment are resident in most homes.

Just as home cooking frustrates the marketing efforts of restaurants, so home schooling frustrates the sales pitch of any conventional school. The more homelike they try to make the school, the more sense it makes to just stay home. Furthermore, just as home cooking has spawned new markets for cooking utensils and cookbooks, so home schooling is creating many new markets for Christian educational products and services. Read *The Teaching Home* magazine and notice the hundreds of advertisers. Thumb through Mary Pride's *Big Book of Home Learning* and discover why it needed to be a "big book." There are hundreds of new companies starting up to serve the home school community. And all the competition means the prices of goods and services are coming down.

Home Schooling Is an Investment

Home schooling is a wiser, more cost-effective approach than other schooling options because every investment made in the home-education program remains as an asset within the household. Most home-school expenditures involve the purchase of equipment, curricula, and basic supplies. These materials are retained in the family's cumulative estate. What would have been a school expense is instead a growing school inventory. Depending on the nature of the curricula selected, textbooks can be held as an asset for use by other siblings or sold for just under their original cost through the home school support group's annual curriculum fair. Recycling the investment results in lower costs for education overall.

Substantial investments made through tuition and fees paid to schools outside the home are not part of the family's household assets; they are true expenses. If the family receives an educational product that is satisfactory, it is a satisfactory transaction; but at the end of each school year, the financial relationship is formally over. School assets are no longer accessible to the family's children or grandchildren, unless additional tuition is paid. School staff, libraries, and facilities are no longer open to the unenrolled students. Lab equipment, sports equipment, and other school property are only available during scheduled periods of time during the regular school year.

Dollar for dollar, not much is left over in the Christian school's budget at the end of the year anyway. Only a minority of Christian schools have substantial accumulations of equipment. The bulk of Christian school tuition generally goes toward paying for school facilities and teacher salaries. (This is, of course, a necessary part of operating any school.) Nevertheless, only a small part of total school income goes toward tangible assets such as school equipment, books, and supplies. Money is tight. Christian schools have managed admirably to provide a better education on a fraction of the budget of the "free" tax-supported public schools. Christian schools do much more with much less. However, the expenses of operating a Christian school are still much higher than the expenses of operating a Christian home school.

Just as the Christian school gets more education out of every dollar invested, so can the home school. Just as the Christian school can offer more personalized instruction in a Christian atmosphere without government regulation of curriculum, so can the Christian home school. Christian home schools offer almost every good thing the Christian schools offer, at a lower cost. They are the logical extension of the Christian school position on nearly every argument.

This "School of Business" is a Real Business

Home schooling allows the family to initiate small business ventures as practicums for the education of children. While these small businesses provide experience and education, they also add to the family's income. It is not unusual to hear of a home-school teenager's college tuition being raised by his own business activities. Due to the federal child labor laws, children cannot be employed in the businesses of others. But they can start their own businesses doing any number of things. Landscaping, secretarial services, commercial cleaning services, and computer programming services have all been successful fields in home-school businesses. Two teenage brothers in one home school reported billing over one thousand dollars per month cleaning aquariums and lobster tanks in restaurants and offices. Their interest in tropical fish has paid off very well.

Net profits do not take into account the value of the experience itself. Home-schooling students can have a resume that far surpasses the importance of a high school diploma. Because the monetary profits underwrite the costs of home-school travel and other study projects, the business activity is a crucial support for the student's entire course of study. One home-school family with five children has arranged to have each of four sons learn a technical skill in the builder's trade (i.e., electrical wiring, heating and air conditioning, carpentry, and masonry). Later, they plan to build one another's houses at substantial savings. Another family has five brothers raising nursery stock. In both instances the older siblings serve as upper management.

Home-schooling families who have family businesses enjoy other advantages as well. Most travel can be a legitimate business expense to be documented for tax purposes. If someone must travel to select and purchase materials for the family business, the trip can be coordinated with other activities with the whole family. Sales calls and meetings with suppliers can make the difference between a pleasure trip and a business trip.

Home schooling and family businesses are not tax dodges or get-rich-quick schemes. Our state and national governments are not anti-business; their financial life-blood is drawn from healthy and prosperous households. Like the local church, the government is a God-ordained institution which prospers only as the households within it enjoy an increase from their labors. That is why the government makes free counsel available to the small businessman, and that is why various tax deductions are given. The home-schooling family, with a going small business venture, can more easily take advantage of these tax deductions.

Some of the financial advantages of home schooling are also available to families who do not home school. Anyone can invest in school materials. Anyone can start a family business. But these advantages can be enjoyed to a greater degree by the family that is free from the constraints of regular school hours.

Because home schooling is a lifestyle, it needn't be seen as an all-or-nothing, take-it-or-leave-it proposition. Making your home a better place for family study and instruction is certainly possible, even if you continue to send your children to a conventional school. After-schooling and summer-schooling are good places to begin. But I hope you will go farther. In the long run, the home-schooling family is far ahead, financially and in every other way.

CHAPTER 29

David Smith's Response to Gregg Harris

EVERY Christian must respect Gregg Harris and others who have sincerely committed themselves to establishing a home school for their children. These parents are not trying to avoid their parenting responsibilities. Indeed, their motivation is usually a selfless love for their children. Unfortunately, what many in this home-school movement have not yet accepted is that if you are in favor of home schools, you don't have to be against public schools.

Sadly, those of us who are involved with, and committed to, public education are viewed by the author as the enemy. The author does not accept public education as an alternative to home schooling that Christians of good conscience would choose for their children. He indicates both a lack of understanding about public education and a lack of respect for the millions of Christians associated with public education.

The author's statements harshly attack public schools but provide little actual information that is helpful to parents. He considers compulsory education to be a way for the "humanistic" public school system to gain control over the minds of Christian students. This betrays a paranoia about the public schools that reveals little understanding of the dedication of public school teachers and a lack of appreciation of public school teachers' and officials' dedication to helping children. The reader is led to believe that humanism and the public schools go hand in hand. This is a gross exaggeration. Though there may be non-Christian views presented in public school classes, generally classes do not deal with these matters, and books and teachers are fair in their approach. Also, he says that children are being socialized by the government. Public schools are local institutions generally and the socialization that occurs is merely the normal and important training of children to function well in respect to other children and adults. Children need to have such interaction to know how to function properly in society, to respect another person's viewpoints, to share, to get along with other people.

The author suggests that public-school children are involved in less serious work than home-school children. He would have the reader think that all children taught at home are academically superior, mature, and have a higher dedication to Christian concerns than their counterparts in the public schools. The implication is that Christian young people enrolled in public school are more frivolous and irresponsible than home-school kids who are thoughtful and more mature. The author's comparisons are self-serving, unsubstantiated, and demeaning to Christian students in public schools. I am sure that both the mature and the frivolous can be found in every type of school, including home schools.

The author considers the public schools a necessary evil. He apparently would be in favor of totally dismantling the public school system. Such a view is a disservice to the many people in this country who greatly need the

public schools. Very few will ever be taught at home due
to the education of parents, working schedules, and the
opportunities provided by the public schools that parents
want for their children, to mention just a few reasons. If
there were no public school system in America, our high
standard of education would quickly diminish to abys-
mally low levels.

Throughout America today, tens of thousands of
local citizens devote countless hours of service in the
sixteen thousand local public school systems. These are
not government schools. These are local schools ably governed by elected leaders all across our nation. These
board members consistently have but one reason for serving—to contribute responsibly to the ongoing improvement of their local schools. Many of these board members
also serve with civic and church responsibilities. If the
author could remove these devoted local leaders from
our schools, what individuals, what groups would he want
to impose upon our communities?

As evangelicals, we all agree that our children's welfare must be a major priority in our lives. Christian parents of public-, Christian-, private-, and home-school children agree that before God they are responsible for the
spiritual, emotional, physical, and educational development of their children.

Christian parents may disagree on the proper kind
of school for their children, but they do agree on the
mandate they share. Each of us as parents has been given
the responsibility to insure that our children receive a
proper education and upbringing.

Mr. Harris has made the commitment of energy,
time, and money to the well-being of home-school children and family living. His sincerity and stewardship are
evident. I admire his dedication. We need more Americans who, like the author, are assertively family-centered.
We differ in that I believe one can be family-centered
and also an active citizen involved with public schools
and other organizations within a local community.

In reading the home-school section, I found that I was in agreement with much that is said by the author. For example, he is against racism; he lists limitations of an age-segregated culture; he believes the home should be the center of life and study; he is concerned with peer pressure and the importance of families participating in activities together. My values and the values of the author are similar. I, too, am concerned with Christian family cohesiveness.

Many comments in the home-school section are true, and we all would support them, but they do little to add credibility to the home school idea; nor do they detract from Christian and public school participation.

I disagree with the author's assertion that home schools are for all Christian students and parents. There are a minority of children and parents who will thrive in a home-school setting. Another minority will be well served by a Christian or other private school; however, the majority of Christian students and parents will continue to select and benefit from direct participation with their local public schools.

I believe in religious freedom for home schoolers and believe in rare cases that home school is an appropriate solution to the educational needs of a child. As a state-licensed attendance officer, I have the responsibility of insuring that all children between the ages of six and sixteen are safe and in some type of school. In a few cases, my contacts with home- school parents have been routine and businesslike. These parents understand my responsibility.

In a few other cases, parents have been suspicious and withdrawn. Last month an evangelical lawyer called me about a home-school case and began to lecture me on the law and religious freedom. He was defensive and simply assumed that I and the school system I represented were the secular enemy. Like this lawyer, Gregg Harris fails to understand the intent of most school officials. Home-school advocates need to understand that, by law, attendance officers need to insure that children are not being abused or neglected by adults. The negative assumptions and defensiveness aimed at public officials are, I believe, rarely necessary.

We read in the home-school section that home schoolers are outgoing and evangelistic. In my contacts with home schools, I have discovered children who tend to be quiet, suspicious, and defensive. This is not the case with every child, but to indicate as a general principle that home schooling produces outgoing children is an exaggerated claim.

I do not want to fight with fellow Christians working in home or Christian schools. I desire peace and respect instead of the verbal attacks, extreme generalizations, and name calling that are now so common. I encourage those whose energies are spent attacking public schools to change their approach. Would it not be better to view public schools as an opportunity for both ministry and service rather than a ubiquitous evil to be both feared and avoided?

If the knowledge and morality of public-school teachers is a concern, I ask the author and all Christians to encourage our best and our brightest to enter the field of public education. Approximately one-half of all public educators now employed will retire or, for other reasons, leave the profession by the early 1990s. This should be viewed as a tremendous opportunity to influence positively our schools.

CHAPTER 30

Kenneth Gangel's Response to Gregg Harris

Even the most casual reader understands the tighter kindred spirit yoking the last two sections of this book. Although Christian-school people and home-school people do not see eye to eye on every issue they might discuss, their educational philosophies derive from a common fount—an unyielding commitment to biblical education.

Mr. Harris enjoys the privilege of defending desirable ground since home school has become the "motherhood and apple pie" of the schooling question in the late twentieth century. Who could disagree with his foundational remarks in chapter 21? It is important to observe, however (and he does not actually tell us this), that home schooling was the only option throughout most of Old Testament history. Furthermore, Scripture does not identify the instructive role of parents in opposition to some other form of education but rather as an ongoing responsibility for all times and places.

Consequently, the Hebrews, fully aware of Mosaic teachings, developed a formal schooling system outside the home. During the fifth century B.C., the synagogue became the central place of instruction in Hebrew theology. Other kinds of schools emerged as a defense against encroaching pagan Greek culture. Elementary schools called "Houses of the Book" were established during the first century to provide formal training for children outside the home.

The establishment of these Hebrew counterparts to Christian schools in no way mitigated parental responsibility nor suggested that parents must be the only faculty under whom children learn. We must be careful not to read into the ancient text our modern ideas of education. I suspect that Hebrew parents living at any time in the Old Testament era would have been surprised to learn that "teach them diligently" implies the use of goals and lesson plans.

All three contributors to this volume would probably agree that the home provides the foundational place of instruction and that parents are the primary teachers. But that is not the question we address in this book. More properly stated we must ask, "Is the home the *only* place of instruction and are the parents to be the *only* teachers?" We can see from the behavior of godly Hebrews and early Christians that they did not so interpret the text. The Hebrews developed synagogue schools and other formal places of instruction outside the home.

The early Christians availed themselves of the Roman public school system, blatantly pagan as it was. They did so because there was no other choice, a reality which still faces many sincere Christian parents in our day. Those who have read the book carefully notice that Gregg Harris and I differ on a major point here. He argues that synagogue schools represented a deviation from the Deuteronomic commandment because they "separated the religious training from economic training." Such a conclusion appears to pass judgment on the text, a judgment completely unjustified by the literature of the Old Testament or extrabiblical materials of the postexilic period.

Whereas the central place of education among early Christians was still the home, Harris is not correct in implying that the education of Christian children seems to have been placed entirely within the home. Just because the word *school* does not appear frequently in the New Testament does not suggest there were no schools. The Christians simply followed the lead of the Jews in making the home the absolute center of education. Nevertheless, schools were important. As Isidore Epstein wrote, school became "an auxiliary home." Nevertheless there were no shortages of schools either in Old or New Testament times, and both Jews and Christians made use of them. (Readers may want to see William Barclay's authoritative book, *Educational Ideals in the Ancient World*.)

In Harris's zeal to defend the home school, he misdiagnoses some cause-effect relationships in education. For example, he cites various important works critical of public education as though they demonstrate the inadequacy of classroom instruction. In fact what they do attack is massive curriculum failure in the public domain and a breakdown of that monolithic system.

The arguments for Christian schools do not revolve around the use of curriculum that integrates the Bible and a Christian world view into every subject. As a matter of fact, most Christian school leaders express discontent with the available curriculum claiming to accomplish this noble goal. We depend not upon curriculum but upon the teachers. Readers will find few emphatic endorsements of curriculum in chapters 11 through 18.

Nevertheless, I am not as concerned with what Mr. Harris says as with what he does not say. He tells us that the home is the most strategic place for instruction, but he does not tell us what the home cannot teach. For example, early education in foundational number and language arts skills can be carried off quite effectively by most parents. Secondary education in sciences, geometry, and literature is quite another question.

Mr. Harris also does not tell us that many parents cannot be effective in home schooling. This is a subtle but extremely important point. He can say, for example, that "the home continues to be the best place for childhood instruction" and as a generalization that may be correct. But certainly not all homes. This fault is common in the literature of the home schooling movement. The capability of parents raises a major problem in home schooling regardless of the helps, curricular aids, and materials now available. The capacity for teaching children at home does not center only on intellectual skills; parents must also be emotionally and socially ready to handle the task of maintaining an efficient home school.

The spiritual qualities of parents will determine whether a home school is Christian or not. Christian leaders commonly complain that churches and parachurch organizations have to take up so much of the slack with children and young people because parents simply do not get the job done at home. Can those same errant parents handle the entire task of education? The responsibility demands much more than the promotional literature suggests. Do not be deceived by subtle implications such as "home schooling is part of God's original pattern for the godly family." True, but not necessarily to the exclusion of other kinds of educational experiences.

Gratefully, Harris has helped us understand one of the best places for home schools—the education of missionary children. The enthusiastic zeal of home schoolers, the viable network they have developed, the increasingly adequate curricular and evaluation instruments may finally help us make a dent in the still scandalous behavior of separating children and parents on the mission field for purposes of education.

However, all of that having been stated, I suspect one of the best Christian alternatives in these chaotic days is a combination of home schooling and Christian schooling. In my view the home school should submit to constant annual evaluation and prepare to give its children over to a Christian school at the appropriate time.

Parents need not be locked into the public school mentality of most Americans. Rather than undue concerns with prayer amendments and the reforming of the public system, Christian educators should design creative and genuinely Christian alternatives. The future is uncertain, especially if anarchy gives way to totalitarianism as Francis Schaeffer suggested it may. But for the moment, parents can choose freedom instead of fear, and parental rather than public control. Christians should exercise their options to the glory of God and the spiritual nurture of their children.

CONCLUSION

Few challenges in life are as momentous as the rearing of our children. A significant component of this challenge is how and where our children are to be educated.

Each contributor to this volume has done his utmost to convince you that his position is the preferable choice. You have seen claims and counterclaims and various arguments, each requiring careful evaluation. You have been asked to weigh the biblical appropriateness of each schooling choice; the educational, familial, and social advantages; the spiritual and financial factors.

Not all of these factors carry equal weight in determining what choice is right for you and your children. Some public schools may not be community-oriented or may promote values that are far from traditional. If you find yourself in this situation, your spiritual and familial concerns will likely favor private Christian school or home-schooling education. You may have inadequate financial means to pay for your children's private education so that public schools provide the only real choice. Or the public schools' superior facilities and technical, vocational, musical, and athletic programs may convince you to choose this educational option. Still again, if you believe the public schools are permeated with humanistic education, your best option may be to take your children from that environment, especially in the earlier years of school. The desire to have one-on-one involvement in the education of your children, closely monitoring the progress of each child, may cause you to decide to educate them at home. If you are a single parent and home education appears to be an impossible task, public or private Christian education may be your choice. As you can see, the possibilities are nearly limitless.

Remember as well that the choice you make may vary with the distinctive needs of each child. And you may decide that one option is good for earlier years and another choice better for later education. Various combinations may work best depending on the uniqueness of your situation.

Only you can make the final determination of where to educate your children. You must weigh the many factors and make your choice. The information presented in this book, along with the counsel of others who know you and your specific circumstances, will give you a helpful start and guide you toward the goal of making a wise decision. Finally, and most importantly, I urge you to pray about the educational choices you face. I'm convinced God will guide you in the way you should go.